Women in Argentina

Florida A&M University, Tallahassee
Florida Atlantic University, Boca Raton
Florida Gulf Coast University, Ft. Myers
Florida International University, Miami
Florida State University, Tallahassee
University of Central Florida, Orlando
University of Florida, Gainesville
University of North Florida, Jacksonville
University of South Florida, Tampa
University of West Florida, Pensacola

University Press of Florida

Gainesville · Tallahassee · Tampa · Boca Raton · Pensacola · Orlando · Miami · Jacksonville · Ft. Myers

 Women in Argentina

Early Travel Narratives · Mónica Szurmuk

05 04 03 02 01 00 6 5 4 3 2 1

Library of Congress Cataloging-in-Publication Data
Szurmuk, Mónica.
Women in Argentina: early travel narratives / Mónica Szurmuk.
p. cm.
Includes bibliographical references and index.
ISBN 0-8130-1889-7 (alk. paper)
1. Women—Argentina—Social conditions—19th century. 2. Women travelers
—Argentina—Attitudes. 3. Sex role—Argentina—History—19th century.
4. Travelers' writings, Argentine—History and criticism. I. Title.
HQ1532. 98 2001   00-053665

The University Press of Florida is the scholarly publishing agency for the State
University System of Florida, comprising Florida A&M University, Florida
Atlantic University, Florida Gulf Coast University, Florida International
University, Florida State University, University of Central Florida, University of
Florida, University of North Florida, University of South Florida, and University
of West Florida.

University Press of Florida
15 Northwest 15th Street
Gainesville, FL 32611–2079
http://www.upf.com

For Moti, Eyal, Martín, and Adriel

In memory of my grandmother Sara Zaritsky de Jaitman

Contents

Figures

Acknowledgments

During the years I worked on this book, I received the support and interest of many people. I thank the Office of Research at the University of Oregon for the financial means to spend two consecutive summers conducting research in Argentina. A grant from the Center for the Study of Women in Society at the University of Oregon made it possible for me to complete the writing of this book. An earlier version of part of chapter 7 appeared in *Monographic Review/ Revista Monográfica* 12 (1996). I am grateful to the publishers for permission to reprint portions of this piece.

I thank my colleagues at the University of Oregon, especially Carlos Aguirre, Barbara Altmann, Jacqueline Cruz, Jesús Díaz Caballero, Juan Armando Epple, Lisa Freinkel, Leonardo García Pabón, Amalia Gladhart, Evlyn Gould, Karen McPherson, Judith Raiskin, Arlene Stein, and Julian Weiss, for the stimulating intellectual environment they provided. The generosity and mentorship of Jaime Concha, Susan Kirkpatrick, and Mary Louise Pratt guided me through the beginning stages of this project. For careful and enlightening readings that challenged my own preconceptions and forced me to reconsider what I needed to say, I thank Debra Castillo, Francine Masiello, Mary Elene Wood, and an anonymous reader for the University Press of Florida. For stimulating questions, I am grateful to Luis Cárcamo, María Elva Echenique, Kate Jenckes, Fernanda Macchi, Silvana Meta, Ana Miramontes, and Raquel Rincón Rodríguez, graduate students I have worked with at the University of Oregon. I thank Amanda Holmes for the very careful translations of the Spanish quotations in chapters 1, 3, 6, 7, and 8, and Suzanne Kocher for the equally careful translations of French quotations in chapter 2. Since I had the final say, any inaccuracies are my own responsibility.

Women in Argentina was written in a continuous and sometimes chaotic flow between Argentina and the United States. I have therefore benefited from the friendship and warmth of those who made me feel at home wherever I was: Ian Barnard, Patricia Chomnalez, Teresa Figueroa, Guadalupe López Bonilla, Claudia Minoliti, Sayo Murcia, María Negroni, Anne Shea, Nancy Solomon, Nora Strejilevich, Rauli Susmel, and Silvio Waisbord. Virginia López Grisolía and Adriana Novoa have been my most constant friends, wherever I am. For her confidence, intellectual guidance, and good humor, I thank Ileana Rodríguez.

This book about the intersections of home, families, and nation owes its largest debt to my own family: my parents, Daniel Szurmuk and Matilde Jaitman, and my grandparents whose choice of Argentina as "their place in the world" has been with me through the writing of this work. Marcelo Bergman's partnership in life and work has been the backbone of this project. Our children Eyal, Martín, and Adriel are present in every page; it is through the rhythms of life with them that I started to think about travel and displacement.

Introduction

As the trees shed their leaves and the heat of summer dies down, children in white pinafores start school in March every year. From March to May, they learn to salute the flag, sing patriotic songs, and dance several traditional dances from the countryside. They are introduced to a 1910 painting by Pedro Subercasseaux that depicts an early 1810s literary soirée at the home of Misia Mariquita Sánchez, and they learn the verses of the national anthem, which Misia Mariquita is singing for the very first time in the portrait.[1] On May 25, they celebrate the birth of the nation in plays that combine references to the minuet-dancing commercial elites of the cities, who are dressed in top hats and elaborate dresses, and the gauchos and *chinitas,* who perform traditional regional dances such as *cielitos, chacareras,* and *gatos.* The gauchos wear boots, the hair of the *chinitas* is contained in long black braids. On June 20, the children commemorate the creation of the flag. For the next month, before the winter break, they paint pictures of the little house in the northern province of Tucumán where independence was proclaimed on July 9, 1816. Inside the house, men in top hats have heated debates on the future of the nation. Outside—the children might imagine—are the gauchos wrapped in their ponchos alongside all the women. Holding babies, nursing newborns, pregnant with the future soldiers of the nation, the *chinitas* and the upper-class women wait. Black slaves light the city lamps and protect the ladies. "Where are the Indians?" a child might ask. "In the desert, in the pampas, in Patagonia, in the frontier," others might answer.

This version of elementary-school enactments of Argentina stresses not only the points of consensus privileged by narratives of the nation but also the points at which the sense of communion breaks down. It is in these points that otherness appears in the form of women, indigenous peoples, blacks, and gauchos. What would a story of the nation that included the alternative narratives of subaltern groups look like? Can narratives of nation include subalterns, or must they always be based on a politics of exclusion and disenfranchisement? These questions lie at the heart of my inquiry into a hundred years of women's travel writing in Argentina.

In this book, I trace the development of women's travel writing in Argentina from 1830 to 1930 in order to show the complexity of women's inclusion in discourses of collective identities. I argue that women—and the feminine—took on different roles at different moments of Argentinean history. I show how white women's access to print culture and political life was argued in terms not only of gender but also of ethnicity. I therefore delve into questions of whiteness and debate how whiteness as a characteristic which was gendered was paramount in the opening of spaces for women's political and cultural participation. Rereading the expansion of Argentina into the frontier that characterizes this historical period, I show how forces of civilization responsible for the creation of the nation were coded as white and female, while the forces of barbarism were embodied by mestizo maleness. White women writers took advantage of their privileged space within the narrative of civilization to intervene into debates of nationhood. Yet they also used this discursive space to criticize key elements of the project of nation building such as immigration policies, emphasizing the places where the new nation would not only enfranchise but also disenfranchise.

This book unearths a rich tradition of travel writing by women. Travelogues on Argentina by French, English, and North American women are read alongside texts by Argentinean women travelers who wrote about the interior of Argentina, the United States, Europe, and the Middle East. I explore the interconnections between personal and collective identities and argue that travel narratives both shape and are shaped by the model of Argentina as a white country. Reading texts by women who belong to different literary and cultural traditions and breaking down the divisions between writers in colonized and colonizing contexts, I challenge the widely held assumption that women's travel writing is a purely personal interior venture, and I show how women used the genre to discuss highly charged political issues. This book not only discusses the relationship between nation building and gender in Argentina but also invites a comparative reading of the relationships of the roles of gender and ethnicity in the creation of print culture in the United States and Europe at that time.

During the period from 1830 to 1930, which marks the transition from independence to modernization, women's roles in society went through drastic changes: women entered the workforce in record numbers and gained access to all levels of the educational system. Women's definitions of self changed in order to accommodate changing social and political realities. My study focuses on travel writing as a genre that requires constant positionings of self in order to document these transformations and account for both continuity and change. While I am interested in stressing the increased participation of women in social and political life, I also focus on the relevance of certain categories such as home, body, nation, and region in travel accounts written by women born in France, England, the United States, and, of course, Argentina. I am interested in sorting out the ways in which these writers discuss belonging and non-belonging, selfhood and otherness. The locus in which these issues are discussed is the frontier, that imaginary space where civilization breaks down and barbarism takes over. The frontier is also the space where the myth of "white Argentina" gives way to the realities of racial diversity.

The categories of civilization and barbarism were brought into the forefront of Argentina's political and cultural life with the publication of Domingo Faustino Sarmiento's *Facundo* in 1845 and are still prevalent in our understanding of Argentinean history and culture at the end of the millennium. In *Facundo,* Buenos Aires and the cities of the Argentinean littoral are presented as beacons of civilization. The surrounding pampas, in contrast, are the repositories of barbarism that threaten the civilizing enterprises originating in the cities. In order for a modern nation to emerge, the forces of civilization would have to defeat the barbaric elements lodged in the pampas, such as the Indians and the gauchos, and include these geographical areas within a capitalist economy. As Francine Masiello has demonstrated in her book *Between Civilization and Barbarism: Women, Nation, and Literary Culture in Modern Argentina,* the conflict between civilization and barbarism was metaphorized in clearly gendered terms. The space of civilization was represented in feminine and ethnic terms with white middle-class women being both the icons of civilization and the creators and guardians of civilized and civilizing spaces such as private homes, schools, and hospitals.

While domestic spaces within cities were the repository of civilization, the open spaces of the countryside were the stronghold of the forces of barbarism. The intellectuals of the generation of 1837 described these areas as dangerous and menacing, the habitat of barbaric masculinity. The countryside was especially dangerous for civilized women: they could become *cautivas,* slaves to the Indians. Venturing beyond the frontier threatened white women's safety. The frontier was the space beyond the ever moving imaginary line where the natural forces of barbarism defied the organizing principles of European civilization. In *El género gauchesco: Un tratado sobre la patria,* Josefina Ludmer shows how the countryside, perceived as the space of barbarism, was co-opted into the nation through the actual enclosing of the land and the symbolic incorporation of the gaucho to the law of the state. Lettered culture mediated this process.

As I have already mentioned, the categories of civilization and barbarism were not only gendered but also strongly racialized. I will argue that the conflation of whiteness with femininity enabled discursive possibilities that allowed multiple substitutions within the discourse of the subaltern with women occupying similar spaces to that of other subaltern groups such as Indians, gauchos, and mulattos.[2] A certain model of femininity, embodied in the white angel of the hearth, made its way into the discourse of nation building within the traditional roles of respite of the warrior and republican motherhood. Male and women writers alike discussed politics within the realm of domesticity. Other aspects of life important to women writers which had no place within family romances, such as desire, work, gender relations, and education, frequently found their way into women's texts through references to the subaltern other. Travel narratives therefore provided the occasion to discuss these other concerns displaced from the actual locations where women lived their everyday lives.

In the first part of the book, "Frontier Identities," which treats the period of 1837 to 1880, I study narratives of the countryside before land enclosures and the extensions of the railroads to show how the space of the frontier coded as masculine is used by women to explore the limits of the liberal modernizing project of the male intellectuals. Women writers such as Juana Manuela Gorriti, Rosa Guerra, and Mariquita Sánchez align themselves at different points with the liberal modernizing project and with those excluded from this project such as gauchos and Indians. European women use the space of the Argentinean landscape to discuss gender relations in their countries of origin, while Argentinean women use Europe to participate in debates on ethnicity and immigration in Argentina. Mariquita Sánchez's personal letters and her memoirs, *Recuerdos del Buenos Ayres virreynal,* discussed in chapter 1, provide a fertile locus from which to problematize women's inclusions in collective identities in the first half of the nineteenth century. Sánchez's writing shows an arduous relationship to her representation by the male writers of the time as the compendia of civilized characteristics. Sánchez's own writing shows how men intellectuals paid lip service to women's rights by insisting on the feminine as a metaphor for republicanism and democracy while they excluded women from the rights of citizenship. In chapter 2, I read Alsatian writer Lina Beck-Bernard's *Le rio parana* (1864), a narration of Beck-Bernard's stay in the province of Santa Fe during the mid-1850s, while her husband was setting up Swiss colonies in the region. Beck-Bernard's text highlights the points of dissension in the discourse of the "white nation" by focusing on the complexity of class and race relations that projects such as her husband's were attempting to erase.

Part 2, "Shifting Frontiers," focuses on women's travel writing during the period 1880–1900. This period is marked by two complementary processes: the massive genocide of indigenous populations represented by the Campaign to the Desert (1878–79) and the establishment of immigration policies to attract millions of European immigrants. National unification and modernization are constructed on the basis of these absences (the Indians) and the hope of the new presences (the Euroargentineans). Women travel writers during this period grappled with issues of resistance to and intervention in modernization. Eduarda Mansilla's *Recuerdos de viaje* (discussed in chapter 3) and Florence Dixie's *Across Patagonia* (discussed in chapter 4) are interventions into the debate on the destiny of indigenous populations and veiled critiques of the Argentinean extermination model. In *Across Patagonia* (1881), for example, Florence Dixie, an English aristocrat, describes blissful marital relationships and child-rearing practices among the Tehuelches of Patagonia. I argue that in her descriptions of the Tehuelches, Dixie establishes an underlying contrast with family relations in Britain: the pastoral image of the Tehuelches she records highlights the problems of family relationships in her native country. Her descriptions also point to a very active and ebullient community life in contradiction with the prevalent portrayal of indigenous communities as already lifeless, condemned, and doomed. During the same period, Argentinean socialite Eduarda Mansilla uses her travelogue *Recuerdos de viaje* (1880) to criticize the model of the Indian reservation in the United States at a time when similar structures were being discussed in the Argentinean Congress. The travelogues by Dixie and Mansilla bear witness to the reality of the life of the indigenous populations of Argentina when narratives of nation were wiping out all traces of their existence. In chapter 5, I discuss *In Distant Climes and Other Years* (1931) by Jennie E. Howard. Howard, a North American teacher imported by Domingo Faustino Sarmiento, documents the creation and expansion of the normal school system in the country. Howard's travel writing marks the emergence of a new model of femininity embodied in an independent professional woman. The shift from Dixie's and Mansilla's texts to Howard's is symptomatic of a larger process taking place at the beginning of the twentieth century: otherness ceases to be represented by Indians. Immigrants, homosexuals, transvestites, mestizos, Jews, and the urban poor take their place.[3] In the imaginary of the nation, the myth of the "white Argentina" emerges with all its force.

Part 3, "Shifting Identities," is devoted to travel narratives by modern women in the modern nation in the period 1900–1930. In chapter 6, I offer a reading of *Stella,* a 1905 novel by Emma de la Barra which became the first best-seller in the history of Argentinean literature. In *Stella,* de la Barra uses the tropes of travel literature to explore the role of white women in the nation. Chapter 7 focuses on two professional women who used teaching within the public school system to legitimize nontraditional lives. Cecilia Grierson, the first Argentinean female medical doctor, wrote a 1902 report for the government detailing her experience as a government envoy in Europe; Ada María Elflein wrote travel articles on the Argentinean interior for the newspaper *La Prensa* in 1918. These women negotiated participation in the public sphere while incorporating the discourse of the white nation into their writing. The pampas for them become a symbol to be included in the narrative of the nation but one that, in reality, is ultimately dangerous for modern women. Delfina Bunge's *Tierras del mar azul* (192?), treated in chapter 8, questions the successes of the modernizing project and poses the religious pilgrimage as the only possible trip for women. The foreign others of Bunge's text—Jews, Arabs, and poor Italians—are also the domestic enemies of the intellectual generation that provided the discursive rationale for the military coup of 1930 which ushered in a period of fifty years of political unrest and drastic social and economic changes.

Travel Writing and Narratives of Otherness

In her influential book *Imperial Eyes: Travel Writing and Transculturation,* Mary Louise Pratt explains the key role of travel writing in the creation of the "rest of the world" for European readers. Travel writing as a genre became increasingly engaged in scientific codification, which in turn legitimized the intervention of Europeans overseas.[4] Although this project was undertaken mainly by men, European women were involved in imperial travel from very early on in the colonial expansion of Europe. Travel writing, like colonizing, however, was mostly a male endeavor. The proliferation of travel texts by nineteenth-century women notwithstanding, an overwhelming majority of travel writers were men, and the genre was defined within marked male categories such as the privileging of the gaze and freedom of movement. European women travel writers had to contend with this tradition and participate in it within the limits imposed by gender. Their interventions were often marked by an emphasis on certain subject matters such as private lives, and feminine spaces such as homes and harems.[5]

In Argentina, after independence, former colonial subjects wrote travel books to narrate their own incursions back into the metropolitan centers. Argentinean intellectuals traveled to Europe as a means of preparing themselves for participation in political life. On their return, they wrote travelogues that documented not only their experiences in Europe but also their participa-

tion in the genre of travel writing. As Noé Jitrik observes, these two endeavors—traveling to Europe and writing about traveling to Europe—have always
been paramount for Argentinean intellectuals interested in entering the public
sphere, since the recognition of Europe is "one of our most impotent traumas"
(*Viajeros* 12). The *initiatic* trip to Europe that male intellectuals took was carefully documented in their travelogues written for publication. As David Viñas
and Adolfo Prieto show, these travelogues were meant to be read dialogically
against each other.[6] In careful detail, writers, politicians, and future presidents
wrote about being reclaimed by mother Europe and rebirthed for success,
modernity, and power.

While travelogues written by men were immensely popular in the new
Latin American republics during the nineteenth century, very few women
writers in Latin America actually published travelogues. Many of them, however, wrote about traveling in different forms. As Susan Kirkpatrick shows in
her study of women's writing in Spain in the nineteenth century, Romanticism endowed women with a "particular kind of subjectivity, one designed for
nurturing children and maintaining the affective ties of the nuclear family"
(*Las Románticas* 25). Within the context of this subjectivity, women writers produced novels and short stories that addressed issues of nation building within the
limits of the bourgeois family. Traveling appeared profusely in these texts because
exile was one of the major issues at stake throughout most of the pre-1880s
period in Argentina. The first travelogue written by a woman to be published
in the country, however, was Eduarda Mansilla's *Recuerdos de viaje,* which appeared in 1880 after national unification.

There is a powerful reason why Argentinean women writers did not produce travelogues. For upper-class women in Argentina in the nineteenth
century, traveling was a mark of class position, and familiarity with European
social and domestic ways was a given. Travel writing requires a positioning of
otherness that these women could not accomplish in relationship to Europe. It
is therefore not surprising that the first travelogue published as such by an
Argentinean woman in the nineteenth century described the author's trip not
to Europe but to the United States. Eduarda Mansilla traveled extensively in
Europe, yet she reserved the genre of travel writing for her experience some-
where else. In Western Europe, she blended in. Being a white woman of the
upper class in nineteenth-century Argentina was synonymous with "passing"
for European. Traveling to Europe was therefore another form of being at
home. Well into the 1950s when Victoria Ocampo writes about her youth in
the early decades of the twentieth century, she reserves the descriptive discourse of travel writing for the working-class neighborhoods of Buenos Aires
while she describes her experiences in Rome and Paris as extensions of her
experience in the upper-class areas of Buenos Aires. Otherness resides in the

borders of the city of Buenos Aires embodied by immigration. In contrast, the world of the French and Italian rich was, for women of Ocampo's class, an extension of home and therefore could not become the subject of travel books. Travelogues on Argentina published by European women were read avidly because they provided a sense of how the mirror project of creating Europe in Argentina was progressing.

In women's travel narratives, we can observe the conflict of identity definition in very specific terms, because writing about travel requires an active engagement with the physical space the writer is observing and describing, and the physical spaces which are kept in mind for comparison. It is a genre that requires constant questioning of motives and positions. Most of all, it forces the writer/narrator to set herself in the role of "other." Yet to transform herself/himself into a stranger, the travel writer also constructs a community of readers who share her/his values and cultural mores. The appeal of travel writing as a genre lies in the narrator's transformation into a stranger. It is also a genre that requires leaving the comfort zone, as it were, traveling to other places, questioning categories which will be critical in this study, such as home, landscape, region, language, and nation.

Otherness

I want to spend some time now explaining how I will use the term "other" in the context of this study. My main premise is that travel writing relies on the existence—real or imagined—of two distinct communities. On the one hand, the travel writer necessarily imagines a community of readers who share his or her values, worldview, language, and an understanding of the landscape. The other community is that of those described who are presented as foreign, with a different understanding of the world and its values, some or major differences in language, and a different relationship with their own habitat.

It is my contention that unless a travel writer constructs otherness, he/she cannot construct the community of readers for her/his text. This is dialectic since the construction of self is generated and reproduced by the construction of otherness. In *Strangers to Ourselves,* Julia Kristeva argues that "[t]he foreigner, as it has often been noted, can only be defined in negative fashion. Negative with respect to what? The other of what group? If one goes back through time and social structures, the foreigner is the other of the family, the clan, the tribe" (95). In travel writing, I want to argue, being a traveler is resignified as being home, as having the authority for writing and describing. Those who are described, in contrast, are the foreigners, foreigners to the community of readers that the travel writer is creating in his/her text.

The creation of the community of readers is fundamental for travel writers because they position themselves in space vis-à-vis otherness. All the writers I treat in this book share an understanding of community of origin that is grounded in ethnicity and class and in the spaces where upper-class white women feel comfortable, mainly urban settings or subdued enclosed nature such as gardens or "estancias." Bourgeois whiteness is the primary signifier in the works of these women, alternatively set up against the realities of indigenous men and women, men of different classes, and the physical reality of the frontier. Since the creation of the symbolic representation of Argentina as nation relied heavily on white womanhood, these women writers had to also negotiate their access to privileged spaces within the nation (in opposition mainly to non-whites and the working class), while uttering a discourse that challenged various premises on which their own privileged status was grounded.

Writing Landscapes/Writing Bodies

Argentinean intellectuals of the nineteenth century, Juan Bautista Alberdi, Domingo Faustino Sarmiento, and Esteban Echeverría, among others, drafted a project of nation which carefully outlined the desirable physical characteristics of the future inhabitants. The bodies of women were, for the "Fathers of the Nation," the vessels for future modern Argentineans: whiter, taller, civilized. Alberdi himself advocated the importation of northern European women who would whiten the native population and in turn educate children away from the recalcitrant obscurantism of Hispanic traditions and religion. For those who did not have a chance of being reconceived and rebirthed, traveling to Europe was the only way to recreate themselves, whitewash their medieval Spanish values and the dust of the gaucho-infested pampas, and come back as quasi Europeans. Travel writing by males therefore relates public life, encounters with modernity, intellectual debates, and, in some cases, the titillating sexiness of Parisian nightlife.

European male travelers to Argentina mostly concerned themselves with the landscape and its economic potential for the metropolis. Patagonia and the pampas were two favorite areas in which to depict the lack of sophistication and technical advances of the natives. Onto these areas, British travelers projected their dreams of progress, looking at a mountain and imagining a functioning mine, gazing down a hill into a calm river and dreaming of an active port crowded with ships and sailors.[7] Accounts of Buenos Aires ranged from despairing reflections on lack of sophistication and cleanliness in the mid-nineteenth century to admiring depictions of modern advances and wealth around 1910. Women got the approval of most of the male travelers; men were mostly discounted as too feminine, too lazy, and too vain.

Travel writing by definition narrates encounters with otherness and requires the positioning of the writer/narrator within the text vis-à-vis otherness. While nineteenth-century male travel writers grappled with issues of control and dramatized these in hierarchical tropes of watching and being watched, women travel writers subverted these tropes by placing themselves within the looked at as much as within the lookers. Florence Dixie's *Across Patagonia,* for example, includes pictorial descriptions of Patagonia which challenged the prevalent modes of representation by including the European onlookers in the representation of an Indian camp. What becomes apparent in Dixie's book is what male travel writers to Patagonia had hidden: the role of the presence of the European observer in the daily life of the indigenous populations. Dixie's undermining of the invisibility of the gaze rests not only on her awareness of herself as an eyewitness but also on her realization that she too is being looked at.

The discussions that follow are informed by the mutual gaze that all these texts share. While male travel writers often position themselves as uninvolved witnesses, the women travel writers I study carefully place themselves within their own narratives. They blur the dichotomy between onlooker and looked-at by placing themselves both as objects and as subjects of the gaze. They also address topics such as domesticity, gender roles, and family relations, which further enhance their own participation in the exchange of gazes. There is a sense in these texts that these women writers describe scrutinizing as much as being scrutinized in the areas of life in which all women are expected to participate. The topics male writers privilege, such as use of technology, immediately require a dichotomic relationship between those who have access to it and those who do not. The emphasis women writers place on categories such as the raising of children allows for diagonal readings of the lives of the community observed and the community of origin. All the women travel writers I study in this book—irrespective of social class, sexual preference, and marital state—choose to universalize categories such as motherhood, motherly love, inequality between the sexes, and the frailty of women's role in society. Within these universalized categories, women travel writers create a sense of sisterhood between white and indigenous women. This sisterhood is frequently extended to male subalterns such as gauchos and Indian men. While I stress certain general identity traits that these women writers share such as whiteness and literacy, I also address issues of difference and access to centers of power. Women writers' constructions of themselves as protagonists of their own narratives foreground their own struggles to articulate multiple differences, not only of gender and nationality but also of region, sexual preference, and ethnicity. It is within this framework of multiple identity constructions that I want to set my discussion.[8]

The women I treat in this work are extraordinary women; they are women who defied established norms of the period and who traveled into *terra incognita* not in their trips but in their excursions into the world of language. I therefore explore the strategies by which they create discursive spaces of home and away that allow them to write accounts within patriarchal norms. "Home" will be one of the critical spaces for the analysis of these texts. Women travel writers negotiate binary constructions of home/away; home/not home. And inside and outside these homes, they place bodies, their own bodies and the bodies of others—poor women, Amerindians, mestizos.

My study traces the connections these women establish between body, home, language, and landscape. I look at the constructions of self and otherness in women's travel writing. I argue that besides being restricted to white women, intervention in the genre of travel writing as genre is marked also along class lines. The women who actually wrote travelogues for publication belonged to the upper class and inscribed their own writing on travel within the tradition of autobiographical introspection. The professional women writers I discuss in chapter 7 use narratives of travel within forms of professional writing and therefore erase their own subjectivity from their texts. I claim, however, that in all these different forms of writing about travel, women writers position themselves within the problematics of defining self and other against the backdrop of the frontier.

Body/Home/Nation

Both body and home have been used throughout the history of Argentina as metaphors for the nation. In travel writing by women, home and body become especially concrete because they are at the very center of women's texts. Yet it is specifically this very concreteness which allows us to glimpse into the countless possibilities for metaphor and metonymy, for, above all, these bodies and these homes were the spaces for the enactment of the realities of the daily life of privileged members of the nation. All the women travel writers I treat in this book had a position of privilege, inherited or obtained through involvement in professional activities.

Feminist scholars such as Elizabeth Garrels, Francine Masiello, Ileana Rodríguez, and Doris Sommer have studied the encoding of discourses of nation building within narratives of gender and domesticity. In this study, I want to examine the complementary process, that is, how women writers' incursions into discourses of politics and nation building are a way of securing safety in the home. Peace in the nation therefore is a requirement for the establishment of bourgeois domesticity. Homes in these texts are always in danger of being attacked, intruded upon, and destroyed. The sense of precariousness of female spaces such as homes and schools, which became so painfully evident during the period of state terrorism from 1976 to 1983, is already present in these much earlier texts.

Feminine Spaces

The frontier is the imaginary space where identity merges into nonidentity and where white middle-class women can become slaves. While this representation of the frontier takes different forms throughout the hundred years I am studying, it is present in these texts as the menacing space of non-belonging where white women are in danger. The struggle between the modernizing or modern self and the regressive other is played out in the space of the frontier, the geographical locus of the other.

The texts I discuss in this book are vital accounts of women pushing the limits of their assigned roles in society. Yet few of them saw themselves as pioneers, and therein lies the attraction of their texts. In a broad sense, they were adhering to preassigned gender roles, while they were subreptitiously using what Josefina Ludmer has called "tricks of the weak" to subvert them ("Tretas" 53). Travel writing as a genre afforded them the possibility of playing against the limits of acceptability while they could still pretend they were simply performing the roles of good women, good mothers, and good teachers.

These three roles—good woman, good mother, good teacher—are a common denominator in the works I discuss. It is from these roles that these women embarked on the trips they would later discuss in their writings. These women, however, do not present themselves as good wives, and they do not present themselves as nation builders. Sánchez, Beck-Bernard, Dixie, Mansilla, and Bunge travel with their husbands who are involved in ventures of politics and business. The husbands are, however, absent from their wives' texts and so are their enterprises. Cecilia Grierson and Ada María Elflein travel in representation of governmental agencies and of a newspaper, respectively, yet they seldom talk about the male figure behind the enterprise. In the space of their works, these women are alone with their pen, their paper, their language.

In their texts, all the women writers I study establish a safe place of authority (which does not defy male authority) and from which they construct their voice. There is a male figure in the background, but in their texts the women are on their own, looking on, writing, bearing testimony to difference and sameness. The landscape that appears in the background is mostly that of the pampas, miles of fertile flat land which by the mid-1830s had been coined as a typically Argentinean landscape by a dozen British travelers and the creole intellectuals who used their writings as model texts. This landscape is as much a thematic marker for the foreign women travelers writing on Argentina as it is for the Argentine-born women authors who write on other geographical areas—the United States, Europe, the Middle East, Brazil.

Coming Home

I have drawn from the work of countless scholars who have placed themselves in the midst of what Sarmiento called as early as 1845 the Argentinean riddle and have tried to make sense of it. I have sought to contribute to this ongoing dialogue situating myself within what is spoken and silenced within it. Hence, I examine the ways in which narratives of nationalism include and exclude gendered, classed, and racialized bodies. I show how descriptions of sceneries are always subjective inscriptions of self, and I read travel narratives connecting discussions of scenery and discussions of subjects.

I started thinking about the issues I discuss in my book in a seminar on writing and imperialism I took with Masao Miyoshi when I was in graduate school at the University of California, San Diego. Texts I read in that class such as Johannes Fabian's *Time and the Other,* Ong's *Orality and Literacy,* Ngugi wa Thiongo's *Decolonising the Mind,* and Edward Said's *Orientalism* made me question my own understanding of the place I grew up in a suburb of the city of Buenos Aires. I demystified my own relationship with the miles of fertile land that I saw when I drove with my family to the beach every summer. As a child, I echoed my teachers' descriptions of the pampas as the source of national wealth. As an adolescent and a college student, I argued for land reform and the expropriation of land. In graduate school in the United States, I came to realize how a cultural construction of the scenery of my birth province had formed my own understanding of myself as a gendered, racialized, and classed member of the Argentinean nation.

I have never spent much time in the country. My family did not own land and we did not know anyone who did. Yet the uninterrupted miles of green pastures enclosed by barbed wire were as much a part of my definition of who I was as the train that runs two blocks from my childhood home (a legacy of British imperialism, nationalized by Juan Perón and privatized by the military junta in the early 1980s and by Peronist president Carlos Menem in the 1990s). Two faces of a project: vast expanses of land, an overpopulated modern city.

The final impetus for the writing of the book came during a celebration of independence on July 9, 1997. My six-year-old son Martín, born in California and raised in California and Oregon, is dressed as a gaucho and carrying the Argentinean flag. He sings to the flag, dances with a little girl with artificial black braids, and shouts "Viva la Patria! Viva la Libertad!" The nation is performed, yet again, within the safe space of a school yard. And, as always, it is intertwined with gender roles, ethnicity, and class. It is in the vague verses of the national anthem forever sung by Mariquita Sánchez, in the colors of the flag, in the particular regional tones of language that enactments of nation defy rational understanding. It is the sense of being home after a long trip and the knowledge that for a few minutes, and in performance, community exists. This book has been written within and against this illusion.

1

Frontier Identities, 1837–1880

1

A House, a Home, a Nation: Mariquita Sánchez's
Recuerdos del Buenos Ayres Virreynal

A few months after landing in Buenos Aires in 1845, German painter Johann
Moritz Rugendas painted a portrait of Argentinean socialite and writer Mariquita Sánchez (figure 1). Hailed by critics as the first Romantic portrait in the
River Plate that incorporates the American landscape, the painting shows
Sánchez sitting on a sofa that merges into a wild yet contained natural landscape.[1] Her black dress demurely covers her body and a white kerchief is on her
lap. This portrait masterfully combines the elements that came to signify early
Argentinean culture. A white woman anchored within European civilization
(her mode of dress and adornment, her sofa), within an exuberant yet contained natural landscape. The conflation of women and nature, the delicate
equilibrium between nature that can be contained and nature that poses a
danger becomes clear in the context of another paintings by Rugendas. In *El
rapto de la cautiva* (figure 2), Rugendas shows the dangers of uncontrolled nature
for white women. Placed in the frontier, these two paintings epitomize the
dangers of the frontier for white women: abduction by Indians, acculturation,
sexual violence.

In this chapter and the next, I will read texts by Mariquita Sánchez and Lina
Beck-Bernard which challenge part of the widely held assumptions about the
frontier. Both Sánchez and Beck-Bernard interrupt the male discourse of the
frontier as the ultimate dangerous place for women. Sánchez shows how instability and danger are also part and parcel of life in cities, and how the frontier could
also be imagined as a matriarchal space of bliss and harmony. Beck-Bernard
protests the unfairness of an order that relegates indigenous peoples to disappear-

Figure 1. Johann Moritz Rugendas. *Retrato de María Sánchez de Mendeville,* 1815. Oil on canvas, 61.5 x 51.7 cm. By permission of the Museo Histórico Nacional, Buenos Aires.

ance. In their works, both Sánchez and Beck-Bernard invoke a more democratic vision of the frontier as a space of exchange and mutual enrichment. Within their bourgeois homes and signifying the future of the nation—white, European, Francophile—these authors utter a mild protest which retrospectively reminds us that capitalism, dependency, genocide, and racism are not inevitable.

Figure 2. Johann Moritz Rugendas. *El rapto de la cautiva,* 1848. Oil on canvas, 44.5 x 53.5 cm.

A House/A Home

In a letter written from her exile in Montevideo in 1842 to her daughter Florencia, who was still in Buenos Aires, Mariquita Sánchez, the most important female figure of Argentinean early republican life, describes political unrest in both Buenos Aires and Montevideo in these terms:

> Aquí quieren que todos perezcan y ni las mujeres quieren que tengan miedo, de modo que es la misma cosa que ahí, con un poco más de libertad. Ayer se registraron varias casas y al que se oculta lo sacan amarrado y le hacen soldado de línea. Todo el día tiros, heridos, guerrillas, privación de muchos artículos, de modo que estoy como embarcada, sin leche, fruta carísima, y todo esto al "ñudo." Ni es mi tierra, ni esto me sacará del "pantano," pasando los pocos años que me quedan en padecer y ver padecer, y ni el nombre de política quisiera yo oír. Así quisiera arreglar mis intereses contigo y vivir en descanso, aunque fuera en un rancho. No tengo ninguna aspiración, ni aún vestirme como gente. Sólo lo que deseo

es tomar una taza de caldo y otra de café, sin que me hagan rabiar y sin asustarme. (Sáenz Quesada 191–92)[2]

[Here they want everyone to perish and they don't want even the women to be afraid, so that it's the same as there, with a little more freedom. Yesterday several houses were searched and whoever hides is tied up and carried off to become a soldier. All day there are gunshots, wounded people, guerilla bands, and we lack many staples, so that it's like I'm marooned, without milk, with very expensive fruit and it all seems worthless. It's not even my country, not even this can get me out of this quagmire, after the few years that I have left to suffer and see suffering, I don't even want to hear the name of politics. So I would like to arrange my interests with you and live in peace even if on a "rancho." I have no aspirations, not even to dress like people. All I want is to drink a cup of broth and another of coffee without it making me angry and without being afraid.]

Sánchez depicts in detail the relationship between the personal and the political, and the ultimate desire for the comfort and protection of home. Political strife had exiled her from her Buenos Aires home, where she had hosted the most celebrated literary soirées of the city. Politics caught up with her in Montevideo, and her house there virtually became a ship: insecure, open to searches, and lacking in fresh food.[3] Her yearning is for the safe space of "home" which a ship cannot provide. Neither her house in Montevideo nor her house in Buenos Aires was giving her this security at the moment. This home stripped to its bare minimum is the "rancho," a place where she would be alone with her daughter, in simple clothes, drinking broth and coffee without being afraid. The reference to the "rancho" is of course a hyperbole: to find "home" on a "rancho," Sánchez would have to give up all her privileges of race and class, and nothing in her writings or in her biographical data indicates that she would have been willing to renounce that which basically constituted her as a person—her class status, her whiteness, and her privileged space in the drama of early Argentinean political life. A drama in which house, and home, family and nation, were intricately connected.

In the period from 1830 through 1850 Argentina was a dramatically underpopulated country, a silhouette, a sparse immensity enclosed by arbitrary borders. Although the country had gained independence from Spain in 1810, since then it had been immersed in civil strife in the fight for a definition of a national project. The period of political unrest in Argentina from the late 1820s to the early 1850s set two ideas in opposition: (a) a liberal idea of nation building based on European philosophical thought and proposed by the intelligentsia and the merchant classes, and (b) a "nationalistic" idea of federalism as social pact with a strong foothold in the land and in idiosyncratic traditions. These opposing ideas were the rallying cries of the two groups that dominated Argentina's political arena during the first half of the nineteenth century: Unitarians and Federals. The Unitarians considered the production of culture and especially literature as fundamental to the process of nation building. They equated the creation of a nation in a vacuum, in a desert with writing a book. For the Federals, who saw high culture as a prerogative of the Unitarians, the only possible cultural expression to call their own was popular culture, the emerging expression of the nonliterate classes (vidalitas, songs, popular poems, and plays).[4]

The most prominent figure among the Federals was Juan Manuel de Rosas, a landowner who governed Buenos Aires and represented the other provinces in international affairs from the late 1820s until his defeat at the hands of Justo José de Urquiza in the battle of Caseros in 1852. Rosas's régime had sent hundreds of Unitarians into exile, among them many of the best-known intellectuals of the generation of 1837. These intellectuals would therefore write the nation *in absentia* using stock images from French Romanticism and British travel literature as their source. Looking back nostalgically at the lost country, they created it, writing down a landscape most of them had never seen. Argentina was the product of an intellectual process of piecing together images and words. The trick was to try to be as different and as similar as possible, different enough from Europe to warrant independence but similar enough to be included in European cultural and political traditions as a peer and not as a subaltern. In this game of mirrors, the writers of this generation used the conventions of Romanticism as a literary movement to write against the geography and anatomy of the country and to imagine it otherwise.

In her book *Las Románticas: Women Writers and Subjectivity in Spain, 1835–1850,* Susan Kirkpatrick shows how Romanticism also provided a venue for women to express themselves. Within the context of this subjectivity, women started to produce literature in Europe and in Latin America. Juana Manuela Gorriti's stories are probably the best exponents of the expression of this female subjectivity in Argentinean literature. Gorriti wrote about the pre-Hispanic past, wars of independence, and violence during Rosas's rule. Her melodramatic short stories provided her with a space to develop her ideas on the role of women in the family and the nation.

The family was used as a metaphor for the nation not only by women writers but also by male writers. Critics such as Doris Sommer and Francine Masiello have analyzed the use of these metaphors from different perspectives. Sommer claims that love stories in the foundational novels of Latin America such as José Mármol's *Amalia* and Jorge Isaacs's *María* functioned as metaphors for national unification and nation building. The erotic tensions that weave these stories together would end successfully in sex and procreation only if the nation came together and provided the desiring couple with a peaceful environment. In Part 1 of her book *Between Civilization and Barbarism,* Masiello explains how the Unitarians in Argentina created a feminized discourse to oppose the masculinist and virile discourse of the Federals. According to Masiello, the generation of 1837 perceived women as a force for resistance to tyranny which acquired a "new symbolic value in building the nation" (23). This codification of the feminine as a space of resistance provided women with a freedom to write much earlier than in other countries. As long as women used the feminine metaphors of family and household, their writing was tolerated, praised, and published, and several women became professional writers who supported themselves financially through their writing.

The Unitarians' emphasis on femininity was coupled with an emphasis on whiteness, and femininity and whiteness became interchangeable metaphors of each other. Whereas white middle-class women became the angels of the hearth, black and mulatto women came to stand for barbarism and for the injustice of Rosas's régime. Women of color were associated with disorder and with the dark forces of society. While this worked representationally, it also worked concretely in terms of the political project of the Unitarians:

> Since their goal was to populate the nation with racially uncontaminated subjects, the bodies of women of European ancestry made their way into nationalist texts, serving at once as buffers between racially minorized groups, who were targets of repression, and as a continental model of citizenry that depended upon its female population for its continuity in history. (Masiello, *Civilization and Barbarism* 5)

For the Unitarians, Argentina as home was a project both of identification and differentiation: a country "like Europe" that would work as a reflection of the best attributes of Europe but that would still be different enough to warrant independent government. The generation of 1837 imagined the Argentinean nation from exile and established a way of writing the country that required both physical and emotional distance. The trip to Europe would therefore become the paradigmatic initiation into public and Argentinean political life. Travel writing was as much about the political and the programmatic plans for the nation as about personal and intimate experiences. The personal worked as a backdrop for the political. Traveling was a male project where Argentinean intellectuals defined Argentinity in contrast to other imagined identities, always staying close to the model of differentiation/identification described above.

Women's national identities in political terms—passports, identity cards—were tied to their male relatives' identities. The definition of home, lodged for men in the tension between differentiation and identification, was even harder to pinpoint for women whose political participation was very limited. In their literary production, middle-class women explored the domestic space representing the space of the nation as an enlarged domestic space complete with fraternal strife.

The novel and the short story, and to a lesser degree the essay, became popular genres for women writers in the mid-nineteenth century. Autobiography and travel writing, immensely popular among men writers of the period, were not genres practiced by women until the very late nineteenth century. Perhaps one reason for this is indicated in Adolfo Prieto's argument about autobiographical literature in the early nineteenth century:

> Los hombres que ejercen el poder por esos años rara vez concluyen sus mandatos y sus delegaciones con el acuerdo de todos los grupos facciosos; y es esta falta de correspondencia entre el quehacer individual y la estimativa de uno o de varios sectores de la sociedad, la que crea, en algunas conciencias, la necesidad de equilibrar la fractura producida. La confesión pública es el recurso habitual de casos semejantes: de ahí que no pueda sorprender el número de memorias que se escriben durante ese período. (*Autobiográfica* 37)

> [The men who exercise power around those years seldom finish their mandates and delegations with the agreement of all of the factions involved; and it's this lack of correspondence between the individual task and the approval of one or several sectors of society that creates, in some minds, the necessity to balance the ensuing gap. The public confession is the usual recourse in similar cases: thus the number of memoirs that are written during that period can come as no surprise.]

Autobiographical writing in the early years of independent Argentina, after the 1810 revolution, did not textualize the private as women's autobiography in Europe did at the time. Likewise, travel writing in the same period served public men with an added space to compare political practices and set forth a model of nationhood. Both memoirs and travel books referred mostly to public life.

Women writers of the period did much personal writing in the form of letters, journal articles, and addresses at literary soirées. Although their novels and short stories were ostensibly written for publication, their personal writing was published much later, and most of it was produced without a clear sense of whether it would eventually be published or not. As a matter of fact, Mariquita Sánchez's *Recuerdos del Buenos Ayres virreynal* was published almost a century after it was written. Sánchez's *Recuerdos* is an effort to document a particular moment in River Plate history. Sánchez intertwines the history of the country with her own personal history. Sylvia Molloy describes the tension between the personal and the historical in these terms:

> A strong testimonial stance informs autobiographical writing in Spanish America. If not always perceiving themselves as historians—the perception seems to wane as generic difference becomes more specific in Spanish American literature—autobiographers will continue to see themselves as witnesses. (*At Face Value* 8)

Sánchez writes from the space of authority being an eyewitness has granted her. Lacking most of the introspective characteristics of memoirs, *Recuerdos del Buenos Ayres virreynal* resembles a travelogue. I will argue that given Sánchez's conflicted identity in nineteenth-century Argentina, it can very well be read as one. In *Recuerdos*, Sánchez creates a community of differentiated readers who are distanced from the people she writes about not spatially but by time. Colonial Buenos Aires is presented as a place other than contemporary (and future) Buenos Aires, and Mariquita Sánchez plays the role of the eyewitness traveler who narrates this place other to her community of readers.

Mariquita Sánchez As Symbol

Mariquita Sánchez is probably the best-known Argentinean woman of the nineteenth century. Immortalized in elementary school textbooks as the first person ever to sing the national anthem, Sánchez has become a synonym of the nation-in-the-making, a local Madame de Staël, an interpreter of the best elements that made the creation of the Argentine nation possible in the postindependence period. The French-inspired Argentinean patriots chose Mariquita to perform the triumphant anthem by Vicente López y Planes and Blas Parera and in so doing destined her to become a symbol of the nation. As such, Mariquita combined European sophistication and upbringing with a birthplace this side of the Atlantic. Indeed, Sánchez was immaculately white, the daughter of a prominent Spanish family who married first an English captain and then a French fortune hunter who later became a diplomat.

Born in 1786, the only daughter of one of Buenos Aires' richest and most aristocratic families, Mariquita Sánchez grew up as an ultramarine Spaniard. Her family was important in the milieu of Buenos Aires' Spanish colonial elite, and during her childhood Mariquita enjoyed the privileges afforded to her as a member of this elite. At fifteen, nevertheless, Sánchez clashed with the establishment and its rules when she petitioned the viceroy for permission to marry her cousin Martín Thompson against her widowed mother's will.[5] Even though there was an ecclesiastical procedure that children could use to resist their parents' marriage plans, Mariquita instead appealed directly to the viceroy. Middle-class Buenos Aires women had enjoyed much more freedom than contemporary women of the same social class in Spain. Some of these privileges were intrinsic to life in the New World: more freedom of movement, more class mobility. The success of Mariquita's plea to marry Thompson exemplifies one of the advantages of overseas life for women: the possibility of exercising their "right to love."[6]

Exercising this "right to love," Mariquita Sánchez married Martín Thompson, who was in charge of overseeing activities in the port of Buenos Aires, in 1805. Their house became a center for artistic meetings after the revolution. In 1826, Sánchez persuaded Governor Bernardino Rivadavia to found the Society of Beneficence, which provided a space for women of the oligarchy to participate in public life well into the twentieth century. The Society of Beneficence became a key element in the definition of Argentine womanhood and took over territories usurped from the domain of the church such as the health and education of women. Sánchez was active in this society until her death in 1868 at the age of eighty-three.

Sánchez's first husband, Martín Thompson, died in 1819 when returning from an official mission to the United States, leaving Sánchez in charge of five children. A few months after her first husband's death, Sánchez married Juan Washington de Mendeville, a French adventurer who later became a French representative to the government of Buenos Aires. Mendeville was much younger than Sánchez, and he was Sánchez's children's piano teacher when they met. Six months after the wedding, Sánchez gave birth to Mendeville's son, creating a small scandal in Buenos Aires society. During much of Rosas's government, Sánchez lived in Montevideo and spent a short period in Rio de Janeiro in preparation for a trip to Europe that never happened. After the defeat of Rosas in the battle of Caseros in 1852, she returned to Buenos Aires, where her house again became a center of artistic life in the soirées she hosted.

Sánchez's contribution to Argentine history both as a member of the Society of Beneficence and as the hostess of famous literary soirées underscores the significance of the project she wished to undertake but never really carried out: writing a history of Argentine women. "Voy a escribir la historia de las mujeres de mi país," she wrote to her daughter in 1852, adding, "ellas también son gente." [I will write the history of the women of my country, they are also people.] Sánchez's project was perhaps too ambitious for the time. Unable to do the kind of writing she preferred, which from what he says in her letters would be either political treatises or historical essays, she settles for this description of the Buenos Aires of the past in *Recuerdos del Buenos Ayres virreynal*. In a letter to Juan Bautista Alberdi, she talks about her inclinations:

> Mi vida es la de un hombre filósofo por fuerza, más bien que la de una mujer, con la desgracia de tener corazón de mujer, cabeza de volcán y no tener la frivolidad del sexo para distraerme. Mis afecciones dispersas por el mundo y en una profunda soledad en medio de la más numerosa sociedad. (235)

> [My life is one of a philosophical man by necessity, rather than that of a woman. I have the misfortune of having the heart of a woman, the head of a volcano and not having the frivolity of the sex to distract me. My loved ones scattered around the world and I find myself in a profound solitude amidst the most numerous society.]

Caught between broad political and cultural interests and the narrow space her society provided for women's public endeavors, Sánchez is trapped between identities as well. The subtext of her discussion of pre-independence Buenos Aires, which I will discuss in the next section, is her knowledge of European ways learned as a European "in exile." Even though Buenos Aires is the place where she was born and where she lived most of her life, she can write about using the years past as the distancing element whereby colonial Buenos Aires becomes a place other than postindependence Buenos Aires.

In Sánchez's writing, the relationship between the public and the private is overdetermined: no domestic life can exist until political pacification provides an adequate environment. Peace in the nation is a prerequisite of domestic harmony. It is in the bodies of white middle-class women that national identity is inscribed and performed. The hopes of the generation of 1837 of "salvar la civilización europea, sus instituciones, hábitos e ideas en las orillas del Plata . . ." (*Facundo* 356) [saving European civilization, its institutions, habits, and ideas on the shores of the River Plate . . .] take form in the private life of a woman who actually realized the dream of becoming English and French while never having left South America. Mariquita Sánchez embodies the allegiance to France and England so close to the heart of the intellectuals of the generation of 1837, and in her marriages she actually carries out the physical blending of herself, a creole woman of Spanish origin, with white men from the admired metropolitan centers. The generation of 1837's dreams of transformation and metamorphosis take place in Mariquita Sánchez's private, yet very public, life. While the laws of the time excluded women from full citizenship, Sánchez acquired, through marriage, nominal citizenship in the two most desired nations of the world for her River Plate contemporaries: England and France. In the European lives of her children, Sánchez vicariously lived the dream of European belonging and recognition.

Ideas of nationality and citizenship were very unstable in Argentina well into the 1880s. For women, national identity was even more precarious since their citizenship was tied to their male relatives. Sánchez's letter protesting Juan Manuel de Rosas's accusation that since her marriage to Mendeville she had become "French" exemplifies this anxiety. In this letter, Sánchez establishes a comparison between her marriage to Mendeville and Rosas's marriage to Encarnación Ezcurra and how women are always dependent on their husbands' political and national projects:

> No quiero dejarte en la duda de si te ha escrito una francesa o una americana. Te diré que, desde que estoy unida a un francés, he servido a mi país con más celo y entusiasmo aún, y lo haré siempre del mismo modo, a no ser que se ponga en oposición con la Francia, porque mi marido es francés y está al servicio de su nación. Tú, que pones en el "cepo" a Encarnación si no se adorna con tu divisa debes aprobarme, tanto más cuando que, no sólo sigo tu doctrina, sino las reglas del honor y del deber. ¿Qué harías si Encarnación se hiciera unitaria? Yo sé lo que harías. (Quoted in *Mariquita Sánchez y su tiempo* 168)

> [I don't want to leave you in doubt as to whether a French or an American woman is writing to you. I will tell you that ever since I married a Frenchman, I have served my country with even more fervor and enthusiasm, and I will always serve it in this way unless it is put in opposition to France, because my husband is French and is in the service of his country. You, who put Encarnación in the stocks if she does not wear your red ribbon, you should approve of me, for not only do I follow your doctrine, but I also follow the rules of honor and duty. What would you do if Encarnación became Unitarian? I know what you would do.]

Here Sánchez explicates the different levels of allegiance women had to observe: loyalty to the cause of their country and conformity to the rules that governed women's behavior and which established women's identity as dependent on that of their male relatives. She can have allegiance to both the "país" where she was born and at the same time show her preferences for the cultural project France represents. If this double allegiance is widespread among the members of the generation of 1837, Sánchez also justifies it in the context of her marriage. She stresses this when she brings Rosas's personal situation into play: Sánchez's respect for her husband's citizenship is compared to Encarnación

Ezcurra's adherence to her husband's policies. Sánchez masterfully alludes to Rosas's reign of terror when she uses the word "cepo" (stocks, an instrument of torture) ironically in connection to Rosas's relationship to Encarnación. The "cepo" functions as an implied answer to the rhetorical question Sánchez asks Rosas at the end of her letter, a question which is left unanswered but to which Sánchez claims she knows the answer. The "cepo" appears in connection to the "divisa punzó" [a red ribbon], which Rosas required be worn to show allegiance to the government—and metonymically to the social order. Here the "divisa" is taken out of the context of Rosas-ruled Buenos Aires and downgraded to the level of a domestic issue, a tug-of-war between husband and wife. The "divisa" is therefore "*tu* divisa," not the symbol of the country but a capricious adornment a husband imposes on his wife as a symbol of his power and of her subservience.[7]

Mariquita Sánchez's double allegiance is extended when she—who has never left the River Plate region—brags to her daughter that Countess Walewska thought she was French:

> La Condesa Walewska decía que no podía creer que no fuera francesa, la primera vez que estuve con ella. Al irme, me pidió de volver a verla pronto y entrando un amigo mío enseguida le dijo: "Yo me figuro que he tratado mucho a Madame Mendeville, tanta es la confianza que me ha inspirado y tanto me gusta su modo y maneras ..." S.S. Vino al soplo y yo tan chocha. Todos sus vestidos, moldes y camareras estaban en mi casa todos los días. (*Mariquita Sánchez y su tiempo* 203)

> [Countess Walewska said that the first time that I was with her she couldn't believe that I wasn't French. When I left, she asked me to come back and see her soon and since a friend of mine was coming in she said to the countess immediately: "I figure that I have dealt a lot with Madame Mendeville, she has inspired so much confidence in me and I like her manner and style so much ..." The countess came to visit shortly and I was so happy. All of her dresses, patterns, and maids were in my house every day.]

Here again nationality and citizenship for women are associated—as in Sánchez's letter to Rosas—with female adornment and with the interior of households and all that they meant for bourgeois women. Sánchez is very aware of the connections between female sexual conduct and the legitimation of government, as her letter to Rosas suggests. In the letter to her daughter above, she goes back to the issue of female decorum (her "modo y maneras") to validate her position as a Western woman. Thus she transcends her identity as "americana" and is able to fit into "civilized" society everywhere.

Fashion and Nation

I have often encountered smirks, laughter, and puzzled looks from Argentineans when I mention that I am working on Mariquita Sánchez's writing. The most sympathetic of my compatriots protest that they never knew she wrote. A discussion follows of how much we all remember about her dress and posture in the famous portrait by Pedro Subercasseaux, which shows her singing the national anthem in a low-cut red dress in the midst of the elegance of her French-inspired house. In countless reenactments of the scene, schoolgirls perform Mariquita Sánchez as the angel of the hearth, the respite of the warrior, the hostess who provided the heroes of the nation with food and shelter. Her active intellectual and political life has been mostly forgotten.[8]

Mariquita Sánchez *did* produce texts, although not political texts as she would have wanted. Nor did she write novels like other women writers of her period such as Juana Manuela Gorriti, Rosa Guerra, or Eduarda Mansilla. The texts we still have access to include hundreds of pages of personal letters, a few poems, memos from the Society of Beneficence, and a short account of life in colonial Buenos Aires entitled *Recuerdos del Buenos Ayres virreynal*. This text will be at the center of my discussion of Sánchez's work. I argue that *Recuerdos* requires the reading strategies more often associated with travel writing since the narrator positions herself in the conflictive in-betweenness that travel writers construct.

My analysis is also informed by Sánchez's correspondence with her family and public figures such as Esteban Echeverría, Félix Frías, Juan María Gutiérrez, Domingo Faustino Sarmiento, and Florencio Varela. Sánchez's writing foregrounds the relationship she has with the city where she grew up: it is the city where she was born but it is also the city where she grew up as a Spaniard in exile. Sánchez writes of Buenos Aires in the interstitial space of not quite being a local and not quite being a foreigner. I want to investigate the ways in which defining herself as an "americana" as opposed to a Spaniard in exile benefited her as a woman, and how the American continent provided her with a freedom of movement potentially inaccessible to her in the metropolis. This tension between societies, nationalities, and, ultimately, worlds defines her writing. The tension is not a dichotomy between Spain and America but a multiple confrontation of subject positions in which Spain is set off against America but also against France and England.

Recuerdos was written for a single reader, Santiago de Estrada, and kept in his family's archives until a descendent with literary inclinations—Liniers de Estrada—prefaced and published it in 1953. Like numerous women in the Americas before her, Sánchez produced a requested text written by invitation, suggestion, or direction from male relatives, friends, or ecclesiastical figures.

Like most of these women, Sánchez took advantage of this occasion to write a text which articulates and presents her own voice and her own contribution to history.

Approaching *Recuerdos,* we must first reckon with the category of "memory" which the title evokes. Autobiographical writing enables a discussion of the personal as recuperated in memory. In Sánchez's *Recuerdos,* the personal is absent. Sánchez does not use the first person and she does not position herself as a participant in the social conventions described. She further distances herself from the events described by omitting the nature of her relationship with the key people in her life, such as her parents and her first husband. This distancing of the events described from the narrator who depicts them is characteristic of travel writing, where the weight of the narrator's participation is her/his role as witness.

Travel writers generally establish spatial contrasts between "here" and "there." Sánchez uses time to construct in colonial Buenos Aires a "there," a place other. I have claimed in my introduction that travel writers need to position themselves in respect to collective identities. In *Recuerdos,* Sánchez's strategy of discussing her childhood in a place that she now recognizes as other requires an articulation of self that shuns her own past and creates her character as an Edenic figure. Although it may be claimed that the past always has the quality of otherness, in *Recuerdos,* the past is a prelapsarian order (and women in this prelapsarian society are proto-Eves). Social construction is presented by Sánchez as key to understanding and creating a landscape. Colonial Buenos Aires is a foreign place for the narrator, who stresses its anomaly, its anachronism as a community caught in the Middle Ages. Mariquita Sánchez is reluctant to associate herself with this community and therefore distances herself textually by presenting her parents and her first husband as strangers and foreigners.

What marks the anachronic quality of colonial Buenos Aires is its treatment of women. Women are confined to the domestic space and to religious norms which derive from the Hispanic past. Sánchez's creation of herself as a "new woman" takes place as she re-creates colonial women as completely foreign and different from her. Let us look, for example, at the way in which she depicts her parents, Cecilio Sánchez and Magdalena Trillo. Describing a visit the bishop paid to her parents, for example, she writes:

> para ir a San Isidro, a la casa de una familia, con quien [el Obispo] tenía mucha amistad. Era Don Cecilio Sánchez de Velasco y su señora Doña Magdalena Trillo, pero, nombrada siempre del Arco, nombre de su primer marido. Esta señora era una notabilidad en aquella época; ocupada sin cesar, en el cultivo divino, en las funciones de iglesia; tenía las más originales ideas. (50)

[in order to go to San Isidro, to the home of a family with whom the bishop was good friends. It was Mr. Cecilio Sánchez de Velasco and his wife Mrs. Magdalena Trillo, but always called "del Arco," the name of her first husband. This woman was notable in that era; constantly occupied with church functions and the veneration of the divine; she had the most original ideas.]

This quotation is included within the chapter on religious life, specifically in a vignette entitled "Incidente del Obispo" [Incident with the Bishop]. What Sánchez is describing is the bishop's visit to her family's weekend house in San Isidro. Yet the description is distanced from Sánchez's life in the inclusion of the full names of her parents with no reference to their relationship to her. Sánchez devotes most of the vignette to the description of her mother and her care as hostess to prepare her house for the arrival of the bishop. The very presentation of Magdalena Trillo as a woman completely involved in issues of religion and worship distances her from the filial relationship with the author. Sánchez omits the parent-daughter relationship and therefore challenges the text's obvious function as family heirloom. The emphasis on her mother's role is in keeping with the text's concerns about women's roles also but further prepares the ground for the development of a relationship between self and other along issues of time and not issues of blood. The narrator in *Recuerdos* is a modern woman, a layperson, independent, with a sense of allegiance and inclusion within English and French societies. The "other" against which the narrator in *Recuerdos* constructs her idea of self is a religious woman who, like Magdalena Trillo, is tied to medieval Hispanic conventions.

Alberdi claimed that Unitarians were a hundred years ahead of their time, Federals a hundred years behind. As a firm believer in women's education and women's rights, but restricted by her position as a woman to certain domestic roles, Sánchez was on a different time line from her male Unitarian friends and correspondents. They envisioned a modern Argentina of the future, inhabited by modern lay male subjects and included within a capitalist system of economic exploitation. Sánchez's plan for the future also had a place for equality for some women. It is, I believe, the men and women of the future who shared her understanding of gender roles, who Sánchez envisioned as the intended readers of her text. Sánchez is therefore creating the past for an audience of the future. In this sense, she is, like the travel writer, a translator and intermediary.

The English Are Coming

La juventud de Buenos Aires llevaba
consigo esta idea fecunda de la fraternidad
de intereses con la Francia y la Inglaterra;

llevaba el amor a la civilización, a las
instituciones y a las letras que la Europa
nos había legado y que Rosas destruía en
nombre de la América, sustituyendo otro
vestido al vestido europeo, otras leyes,
a las leyes europeas, otro gobierno, al
gobierno europeo.

Facundo 357

[The youth of Buenos Aires carried with it this fertile idea of a fraternity
of interests between France and England; it maintained a love for civilization, for the institutions and the literature bequeathed by Europe and
that Rosas was destroying in the name of America, substituting other
clothing for the European style, other laws for the European ones, another government for the European one.]

Although Sánchez's text is entitled *Recuerdos,* the narration assumes a certain
distance more characteristic of anthropological or journalistic studies. The autobiographical pact is there: we are to assume that there is an identity between
narrator and author and that the narrator's authority derives from her position
as witness. In this sense, the text can be read as a travelogue in which distance
is not established by a spatial displacement but rather by a temporal one. Like
many travel writers, Sánchez selects different areas of interest and develops
them. As with most women travel writers, these areas of interest are well
grounded within discourses of the private and personal: insides of houses,
schools, churches. The stock arrival scene of travel writers, the moment in
which the immanence of time in the periphery becomes interrupted and included within the historical time of the metropolis, is marked by the arrival of
the English soldiers who invaded Buenos Aires twice in the first decade of the
nineteenth century.

In the description of the invasions, Sánchez clearly marks the difference
between the male "plumas aventajadas" who will write the historical account
and her contribution which is confined to the interiors of houses where the
English soldiers are received socially and the beautiful spectacle they offer when
they march along the streets of Buenos Aires in gallant military attire. The
invasion, which Sánchez's husband Martín Thompson was in charge of crush-
ing, is described as a social visit. The inhabitants of Buenos Aires are awakened
from their peripheral and allochronic existence by the incursion of the British
who while on a military mission also perform "civilization." In Sánchez's text,
civilization is described in terms of physical appearance—that is, whiteness—
and also dress. Fashion becomes a marker of civilization.

Mary Louise Pratt has explained that travelogues include a stock arrival scene which is a trope in the "language of conquest" ("Scratches" 35–37). These scenes stress European intervention as encounter and exchange rather than invasion and conquest. Sánchez reverses this process and turns an invasion into little more than a social visit. The chapter which describes the first English invasion of 1805 starts with the admonition:

> Te he dado una ligera idea del estado de Buenos Aires a la llegada de Beresford y, aunque plumas aventajadas, han escrito sobre esto, voy a darte mi opinión (63).

> [I have given you a small idea of the state of Buenos Aires upon the arrival of Beresford and, although superior pens have written of this, I will give you my opinion.]

This chapter begins by ostensibly evoking Santiago de Estrada, the man for whom the text was written. Sánchez refers to his interlocutor very seldom in her text, and most of the references happen within this chapter. The fact that the previous five chapters are presented as setting the scene for this development is also suggestive. The previous chapters are narrated within the allochronic time of the periphery: life is repetitious and nothing much happens. The arrival of the English marks the entrance of Buenos Aires into modern historical times, and the English, as written by Sánchez, are here to perform modernity and free enterprise. It is not surprising, therefore, that Sánchez reminds us that the invasion interrupted the performance of Moratín's *El sí de las niñas* (a play about the marriageability of a group of young women) that the viceroy was attending at the theater. Again marriage, domesticity, and nation are irrevocably connected.

The first vignette in this chapter finishes with the British flag in the fort of Buenos Aires, the second vignette in the chapter, "Las milicias porteñas y las inglesas," provides an extended description of the physical characteristics and attire of the English and *porteño* soldiers. Let us compare descriptions:

> Permite una disgresión, te voy a pintar estas dos fuerzas militares, una delante de otra. Las milicias de Buenos Aires: es preciso confesar que nuestra gente del campo no es linda, es fuerte y robusta pero, negra. Las cabezas como un redondel, sucios; unos con chaqueta, otros sin ella; unos sombreritos chiquitos encima de un pañuelo atado en la cabeza. Cada uno de un color, unos amarillos, otros punzó; todos rotos, en caballos sucios, mal cuidados; todo lo más miserable y más feo. Las armas sucias, imposible dar ahora una idea de estas tropas. Al verlas aquel día tremendo, dije a una persona de mi intimidad; sino se asustan los ingleses de ver esto,

no hay esperanza. Te voy a contar lo que entraba por la plaza: el regimiento 71 de Escocés, mandado por el general Pack;las más lindas tropas que se podían ver, el uniforme más poético, botines de cintas punzó cruzadas, una parte de la pierna desnuda, una pollerita corta, unas gorras de una tersia de alto, toda formada de plumas negras y una cinta escocesa que formaba el cintillo; un chal escocés como banda, sobre una casaquita corta punzó. Este lindo uniforme, sobre la más bella juventud,sobre caras de nieve, la limpieza de estas tropas admirables, ¡qué contraste tan grande! El regimiento del Fijo, conservaba aún en Buenos Aires toda la vieja costumbre de: coleta larga, casaca azul; todo esto ya era muy usado. El regimiento de Dragones era más a la moda. Pero todo, un gran contraste, sobretodo en la frescura de los uniformes y en la limpieza de las armas. Todo el mundo estaba aturdido mirando a los lindos enemigos y llorando por ver que eran judíos y que perdiera el Rey de España, esta joya de su corona; ésta era la frase. Nadie lloraba por sí, sino por el Rey y la Religión. (65–66)

[If you will allow for a digression, I will describe these two military forces, one after the other. The military of Buenos Aires: I must confess that the people of our countryside are not attractive, they are strong and robust, but black. Their heads are like a circle, they are dirty; some have jackets, others do not; some wear tiny little hats on top of a handkerchief tied around their heads. Each of them is of a different color, some are yellow, others bright red; all of them are broken, on dirty horses, badly cared for; everything is completely miserable and ugly. The dirty weapons, it is impossible now to give an idea of these troops. When I saw them on that amazing day, I said to a close friend: if the English are not scared when they see this, there's no hope. I will tell you what entered the square: the regiment 71 in kilts, sent by General Pack; the most beautiful troops that you could imagine, with the most poetic uniforms, boots with bright red ribbons in the form of a cross, a part of their legs naked, short skirts, tall caps, everything made from black feathers and a Scottish ribbon that formed a hatband; a Scottish shawl as a sash, over a short little bright red frock coat. This attractive uniform clothed the most beautiful youth, of white faces, the cleanliness of these admirable troops, what a huge contrast! Even in Buenos Aires, Fijo's regiment preserved the old custom of long pigtails and blue frock coats; all of this was already very much out of date. Dragones' regiment was more in line with the fashions. But all of them were a huge contrast, especially in the freshness of the uniforms and in the cleanliness of the weapons. Everybody was stunned to see the attractive enemy and crying to see that they were Jews and that they would lose the King of Spain, this jewel of a crown; this was the phrase. Nobody cried for themselves, but rather for the King and the Religion.]

In Sánchez's description, modernity, femininity, beauty, and grace are connected to the English. The gauchos are irremediably relegated to the past by their anachronistic physical appearance and by their attire. The English, in contrast, perform the future of the nation by the mere appearance of their bodies and by the clothes they wear. Discussion of soldiers' appearances will reappear in the narratives of other travel books I discuss in this book such as Lina Beck-Bernard's *Le rio parana* and Eduarda Mansilla's *Recuerdos de viaje*. These writers' obsession with dress and style is associated with the dichotomy between civilization and barbarism, which is developed here. Like a fashion commentary for a women's magazine, Sánchez's discussion of dress is detailed and enthusiastic. Her admiration of the British troops and the "civilized" Europe they stand for is unrestrained. Her only reservation in watching the "lindos enemigos" is that they are Jews, infidels trying to snatch a jewel—albeit an unsophisticated one—from the king of Spain and the Catholic religion.[9] The description of the "gauchos" to whom she herself has referred as "la clase más injuriada" [the most abused class] in a previous chapter of her *Recuerdos* (32) is charged with racism. The insistence on their darkness and dirt approaches an animalization that is confirmed when she jokingly refers to their frightening nature.[10]

After describing the troops' attire in detail, Sánchez describes women's attire in equal detail. While the British troops' dress is adequate, the dress of "las elegantes de aquel tiempo" [the elegant ones of that time] is described as inadequate, too revealing and "insolente" [insolent]. Those in charge of judging the adequacy of women's dress are none other than the British soldiers:

> Que se juzgue lo que pensarían los ingleses en una nación que no se dicen medias y, para colmo, los recibían en los cuartos, con camas muy adornadas con colchas bordadas y sábanas con encajes, riéndose a carcajadas y tomando por sordos y tontos a todos ellos, porque no sabían hablar español. ¡Dios mío! cuando pienso en esto todavía me da vergüenza. La oficialidad que vino en esa expedición, era muy fina, así empezaron a visitar en las casas y a conocer la fuerza de la costumbre o la moda y reírse, unos y otros, del contraste. (69)

[Imagine what the British would think in a nation where no one speaks with reserve and, to make matters worse, they were received in their bedrooms, with very ornate beds with embroidered bedspreads and laced sheets, laughing out loud and taking them for deaf and stupid because they didn't know how to speak Spanish. My God! When I think of all of this it makes me embarrassed. The official who came on that expedition was very fine, so they began to visit the houses to get to know the strength of the custom or the style and to laugh, with one another, about the contrast.]

This friendly description of invasion as social visit and as an occasion for social interaction sets the tone for the ending: Sánchez never refers to the second British invasion, although she does mention that "[v]ino la segunda lección y fue mayor el adelanto. Ya este pueblo conoció lo que podía hacer y pensó en sí mismo" (70). [the second lesson came along and the progress was greater. Now these people knew what they had to do and thought about themselves.] Independence from Spain is therefore implied but never mentioned. Even the relationship between invader and invaded is represented within the context of life inside the houses, inside the bedrooms.

As was mentioned before, Sánchez's description of the porteñas positions them in a prelapsarian state, innocent temptresses with

[l]os brazos desnudos, en todo tiempo, y descote, una mantilla de blonda y un aire, que se llamaba gracioso, de cabeza levantada, que ahora se diría insolente y todas eran muy inocentes. (69)

[nude arms the whole time and low cut dresses, a blond headdress and an air that they called charming with elevated heads, that would now be called insolent and all of them were very innocent.]

This description to some extent follows the paradigmatic descriptions of women by male travelers who represent native women as unaware of their seductive powers, too naked and too forward. Nonetheless, Sánchez, the proto-feminist, echoes European nineteenth-century feminist concerns that women's authority was undermined through overt sexualization of dress. According to early feminist thinkers, women had to learn to become less visible physically and to sublimate their sexuality in order to shed their subservient roles. Sánchez's model of new womanhood is constructed on her own persona: a European in America, a white woman who aspires to participation in the political life of Argentina but who also holds on to the racist ideologies of her European ancestors to justify her own privileged space in the New World. Sánchez's privileging of Europeanness is clear in her admiration of the British soldiers:

Así, al ver a los ingleses tan bien uniformados y hacer sus maniobras como era regular, los admiraban y había una gran concurrencia todos los días, al punto que empezaron a conocer muchas fisonomías de los ingleses. (67)

[So, upon seeing the English so well dressed and doing their maneuvers as usual, they were admired and there was a great turnout every day, to the point that they began to recognize many physiognomies of the English.]

Writing of Self and Beyond

Sylvia Molloy has pointed out that autobiographical writers in Argentina during the nineteenth and early twentieth centuries stress their own position within the history of the country. These writers create a link between the nation and their families, a link that for most writers of the nineteenth century in Argentina was strong and binding. In *Recuerdos*, Sánchez executes the opposite gesture: she opens a gap between herself and her family and creates the persona of a modern woman that links past and future irrespective of the family connections between the past and the future of the homeland. As I will show in the next few chapters, this gesture is shared by other women travel writers: in traveling, these women envision themselves as pioneers, independent from family connections. In writing about these trips, they create a new model of womanhood: independent and self-reliant. This model of travel writing, I will show, will be consistent in depictions of female travelers well into the twentieth century.

In her letters to her children, Sánchez critiques the Unitarians' plans to exterminate the indigenous population and substitute it with European immigrants. This plan, which she opposes, will actually be carried out by her friends once they accede to power after the battles of Caseros and Pavón. While Sánchez critiques this policy, she offers no alternative to the model of a white society championed by Alberdi and Sarmiento except as a utopian reality of life in the frontier that she mentions in her letter to her daughter, quoted at the beginning of this chapter. The countryside that Sánchez longs for is a literary creation, the pastoral illusion found in Romantic literature and not the messy reality of living in a country in-the-making. In this context, it is not surprising that Sánchez imagines drinking coffee and broth and not *mate* (a traditional Argentinean drink), even if she does envision the possibility of living on a "rancho."

The frontier in Sánchez's *Recuerdos* is temporal. The time of colonial Buenos Aires is irrecoverable. The distance between the past—colonial Buenos Aires —and the future—the modern white nation—is lodged in her text by a narrator who has visited the past and can look into the future. And both past and future are possible only within urban spaces. The countryside is condemned to the allochronic time of the periphery and can therefore be narrated only as a disappearing reality. Sánchez's trust in the future of the modern nation is underscored by her belief that the landscape could be controlled and dominated. In this context, a "rancho" could become a home, the pampas could become an enclosed garden, and the city of Buenos Aires could become a bustling, elegant metropolis—a place where a well-dressed British soldier could just blend in.

2

Queen of the Interior: Lina Beck-Bernard's *Le Rio Parana*

Long after returning to Europe, Lina Beck-Bernard used her recollections of life in the Argentinean littoral province of Santa Fe to write a love story located in the open space of the pampas. Her novel, *L'estancia de Santa Rosa,* narrates the unfortunate love story between Mercedes, the daughter of the "estanciero," and José, the son of an Indian servant.[1] The love between Mercedes and José is never consummated: José is killed during an Indian incursion and Mercedes becomes a nun. This love story, like many other women-authored texts, offers an alternative to the narrative of rape as the only possible relationship between white women and Indian men on the frontier.[2] In conceiving of different narrative roles for Indian men, these women writers are also offering their women protagonists alternative subject positions in their texts. When a white woman falls in love with an Indian man, she undermines the patriarchal norms that use white women (and their virtue) as units of exchange and legitimation for white families. The very possibility of "mestizaje" challenges the patriarchal order and the model of the emerging Argentinean nation that imagines itself as white. Using an Indian man as a protagonist challenges his usual position as an antifigure within nineteenth-century French literature.[3]

Lina Beck-Bernard was born in Bitschwiller, a small town in Alsace, in 1824, to a bourgeois Protestant family. Her great-grandfather, Conrad Pfeffel, had been a major figure in Alsatian literature of the eighteenth century. During her childhood, Lina had the occasion to meet her great-grandfather's intellectual friends who had gone into exile in Alsace, such as Madame de Staël and Camille Jordan.[4] When Lina was sixteen, her family moved to Switzerland where she studied penal law. She married Swiss businessman Charles Beck-Bernard in 1852, the year Rosas was defeated in the battle of Caseros by Justo José de Urquiza.

The defeat of Rosas opened the door for the long-desired Unitarian plan to settle northern European immigrants. The first attempts at agricultural colonization in Argentina took place in 1823, but it was only in the late 1850s after the defeat of Rosas that successful colonization projects took place. During the period of 1852–70, however, disputes between Buenos Aires and the rest of the country, and the 1865–70 war against Paraguay, slowed European immigration to the colonies, and it was only in the 1870s that the movement gained momentum.

Charles Beck-Bernard was an early player in agricultural colonization. Soon after the battle of Caseros, he established a company in Basel to organize Swiss immigration to the littoral province of Santa Fe. He first traveled to Santa Fe in 1856 and moved his whole family there in 1857. The Beck-Bernards lived in the capital city of Santa Fe during the period 1857–62. Charles was busy organizing "Colonia San Carlos" (named in imperial fashion after himself) and helping establish Swiss families in the rural areas of the province. He was also writing on the economic prospects of the country and publishing articles and books on the region in French and German. Lina, on the other hand, used the opportunity to compose a charming travel book in which the plans of her husband and his vision for the future of Argentina are absent. This travel book, *Le rio parana* published in Paris in 1864, addresses issues of gender by focusing on the role of women in the new republic.

Le rio parana: Cinq années de séjour dans la république argentine narrates the long ocean voyage to Argentina and provides a summary of Beck-Bernard's five years in Santa Fe. The book was translated by José Luis Busaniche and published in Buenos Aires in 1935 as *Cinco años en la confederación argentina 1857–1862.* Busaniche's title reflects two changes from the original: he uses the term "confederación argentina" [Argentine confederation], which is more historically accurate. In 1854, Buenos Aires severed all links with the provinces and established its independence, while the provinces formed the Argentine Confederation with its capital in Concepción del Uruguay under the presidency of Justo José de Urquiza. With the defeat of Urquiza by Buenos Aires governor Bartolomé Mitre in the battle of Pavón in 1861, the Argentine Republic finally became a political entity and the constitution which had been drafted in 1853 after the battle of Caseros was ratified. Busaniche also includes the exact dates of Lina Beck-Bernard's stay in Argentina in the title. Those dates are not provided in the title of the French edition nor anywhere else in the text. The narrative starts *in medias res,* with the family in Southampton waiting to board a ship. Beck-Bernard provides the exact date (January 9), but the year is given only as "185...." The dates given in Busaniche's translation acquire great significance if read in the context of

Argentinean history: Beck-Bernard's travelogue documents the critical moment at which the landscape of the Argentinean littoral was codified as the progressive mecca of navigable rivers and desirable immigration. The province of Santa Fe was the center of immigration and agricultural colonization during the period 1870–95. Its population grew 345.7 percent during this twenty-five-year period, and by 1895, 41.9 percent of the inhabitants of the province were foreign-born and an additional 25 percent were children of foreign-born inhabitants (Stolen 38–39).

Le rio parana discusses immigration and colonization from the perspective of gender. The most lively descriptions are devoted to the lush landscape of the region, and to female figures that Beck-Bernard either meets or hears about during her stay. Race is also discussed in connection to gender. The displacement of gauchos and Indians, which was required for the establishment of the agricultural colonies, is presented, as I will show below, in connection with the instability of gender roles. Like other women travel writers, Beck-Bernard highlights the continuities between the situation of women in Europe and that of white women in Argentina. There is also an underlying critique of the position of less privileged women—Indians and mestizas—and of subaltern males—gauchos and Indians—who are feminized. The connection between Charles Beck-Bernard's colonizing project and the ongoing uprooting and elimination of Indians and gauchos is more evident if we remember that some of the lands awarded to the colonies were still owned by Indians and that the colonists were in charge of establishing frontier posts to keep gauchos and Indians out and to mark the "civilized" areas.[5] After his eight-year stay in Argentina finished unsuccessfully, Charles Beck-Bernard returned to Europe where he held a political post as a representative of the Argentine government in matters of immigration until his death. Whereas Charles Beck-Bernard shows himself in his own writing to be a very active and willing participant in the creation of modern Argentina, his wife depicts herself as an innocent observer, a visitor who reports on Argentina *as she saw it* but who had no influence whatsoever in what it was to become. In her book, Beck-Bernard narrates what she "sees," describing the present with no reference to what the future might hold for the country if her husband's enterprises succeed, and she never mentions the way in which she is indirectly related to these enterprises. Lina Beck-Bernard dissociates herself and her writing from her husband's project.

It is understandable that for Beck-Bernard as a Romantic writer, direct ties to the project of modernization her husband represented were, to say the least, uncomfortable. She therefore ignores this connection, and the conditions of production of the text are never made overt. We never hear how Beck-Bernard got to Argentina or how long she was there. Even though the beginning of the book suggests that this is a narrative *in medias res,* the missing elements are never provided. The book itself shifts back and forth between being a collection of personal impressions on life and travel in Argentina and an analysis that aspires to ethnographic validity. It takes more than seventy pages to get to Argentina since the author gives detailed descriptions of the trip and of the places visited on the way (Galicia in Spain, Lisbon in Portugal, Rio de Janeiro and Bahia in Brazil). Even Buenos Aires, which is not the final destination of the traveling party, is described in great detail. Once the travelers arrive in Santa Fe, the chronological narration is replaced by typified descriptions of scenery and people with the titles of chapters defining a particular topic (for example, "le 25 mai," "la fête de nuestra señora du Guadeloupe").

In the first chapter we find out that the narrator is traveling with her husband, her children, and a "femme de chambre" described as "courageuse" and "utile." The husband and children do not get adjectives. In fact, they are scarcely included in the narrative at all: the husband is camouflaged in the "nous" Beck–Bernard constantly uses, while the children are mentioned in passing in a very few instances in which reference to them is needed to make a certain point. We do not know how many children there are. We do not know their ages, genders, names. We never find out that two of Beck–Bernard's children died in Argentina nor how this affected their mother. Reading this book, it is difficult not to imagine that its sole purpose was to give Beck–Bernard free rein to express herself outside of the constraints of her role and position within her family and society.

Throughout the book, she exercises her observational ability in descriptions, narratives, and anthropological, ethnographic, and historic discourses. She is well versed in Argentinean history, and she offers extensive descriptions of Rosas, his government, and the character of his daughter Manuelita. Beck–Bernard starts off as a very participatory narrator: her voice is personal and even introspective, her descriptions are flowery and rich. There is something intriguing about the fact that she seemingly acquires a voice from traveling, from her very displacement. What is lacking is a self-reflective element that tells us precisely how this voice came into being and how this first person plural point of view came to be constituted. By the end of the book, Beck–Bernard's voice becomes more feeble, she quotes extensively, and her own perspective is lost. Her departure from the country is not narrated, her personal narrative is cut short, and the book finishes with a description of Indians of the Argentinean littoral which includes full pages of verbatim quotations from the Franciscan monk Constance Ferrero y Cavour and, later, a biography of the monk himself. The book finishes at this point, and Beck–Bernard's voice never reappears to bid farewell to her readers.

The ease with which *Le rio parana* flows, the quality of the narrative, raises the issue of how long Beck–Bernard had hoped for a chance to write. Beyond any writing on Argentina and its scenery, the book functions as a space where Beck-Bernard can write (about) herself. What seems crucial is the writing: beyond anything that Beck-Bernard is writing about, she is exercising her pen. The numerous descriptions that precede her stay in Argentina are exactly that: Beck-Bernard exercising her pen and her subjectivity in a genre that does not compromise her as a woman or as a mother. And in her exercise, she also includes her own sometimes untraditional and progressive political views.

Women writing in colonial situations rarely have agency. If they do, this agency is often derived from a man's: that of a husband, a father, a brother. Beck-Bernard makes no use of whatever agency she might have drawn from her husband, although it may easily be argued that her very act of writing is derived from her husband's and her great-grandfather's influence. She erases the position of power she held in Argentinean society as Beck's wife. She puts this relevant position aside. Her portrayal of herself shows her as an outsider who can "blend in," an unusual position for an educated French woman writer in the provincial Santa Fe of the mid-nineteenth century.

Scholarship on women writing about empire has usually concentrated on the dichotomy "collaboration versus resistance" and has tried to decide whether a particular woman writer at a particular time was resisting or collaborating in the colonial enterprise. Beck-Bernard's book seems to preclude this kind of analysis: she removes herself from the site of conflict, erases her relationship to positions of power, and creates an alter ego that is not related in any way to male endeavors such as the creation of a colony—or to the creation of a nation. Her alter ego is a woman without a past and with no reason to be where she is. In her text, she is free and alone but still respectable, guarded as she is by the figure of a husband and children included in the "nous."

Queens of the Pampas

Women are the focus of *Le rio parana,* and Lina Beck-Bernard's discussions of gender are always informed by her understanding of race. Most of her characters are female, and her depictions of the stock figures of nineteenth-century travel writing on Argentina—gauchos and Indians—are presented in connection with women (that is, mestizas and Indian women as mothers) or to gender (that is, gauchos and Indians as feminized). In this context, it is not surprising that her discussion of the figure who most captured the attention of Europeans—the gaucho—is preceded by the presentation of a woman disguised as a gaucho:

Je dois à la fille du général Stanislas Lopez, doña Mercedes Lopez de C★★★, quelques détails assez intéressants sur Manuelita, qui était unes de ses amies d'enfance. Elles sortaient souvent à cheval ensemble, Manuelita habillée en *gaucho,* pour obéir aux bizarres caprices de son père. Ce serait peut-être ici le moment de dire ce qu'est le gaucho et ce qu'il était sous Rosas. Le gaucho représente dans la confédération argentine l'élément rétrograde. (92)

[I owe the daughter of General Estanislao López, doña Mercedes López de C★★★, some very interesting details about Manuelita, who had been one of her childhood friends. They often rode together, Manuelita dressed as a *gaucho* to obey her father's bizarre whims. This would probably be the place to explain what the gaucho is and what he was for Rosas. The gaucho represents the retrograde element within the Argentinean Confederation.]

In most travel narratives of the period, the gaucho is introduced as a source of danger—a menacing dot on the horizon. In *Le rio parana,* being a gaucho is presented as a performance, a masquerade, not unlike the figure of the stock gaucho of elementary-school plays I discussed in the introduction. The paradox that Beck-Bernard writes into her presentation of Manuelita performing as a gaucho—"obéir aux bizarres caprices de son père" [dressed as a *gaucho* to obey her father's bizarre whims]—is that while Manuelita's performance of barbarian masculinity was used by Argentinean Unitarian male writers to mark the fierceness of régime which could not protect white womanhood, Beck-Bernard's also marks the unfairness of the discourse of the Unitarians toward nonwhites. In this way, Beck-Bernard's text comes close to deconstructing one of the basic premises of the discourse of Romanticism within which the text is written. Following Cora Kaplan, we must remember that modern feminism and cultural theory "emerged as separate but linked responses to the transforming events of the French Revolution" (150). According to Kaplan, "[t]he autonomy of inner life, the dynamic psyche whose moral triumph was to be the foundation of republican government, was considered absolutely essential as an element of progressive political thought" (151). This emphasis on inner life which welcomed white middle-class women into writing also excluded from subjectivity others in terms of race and class. The connections between the multiple exclusions are in the background of Beck-Bernard's text. The privileged space that white creole women held as the vessels of the future white citizens and as creators of a European space in exile is presented in the context of their difference from the Indians whose precarious situation is metaphorized in their feminization. The Indians are the inhabitants of the desert, whereas white women are the "queens of the interior":

A peu d'exceptions près, les femmes sont les reines de leur intérieur, et excercent cette royauté d'une façon peu constitutionnelle, ce qui faisait dire à un Gênois marié à une créole: "On peut penser de ce pays ce que

Machiavel écrivait d'une ville républicaine de l'Italie:—'C'est le paradis des femmes, le purgatoire des hommes, l'enfer des bêtes.'" (*Le rio parana* 132)

[With few exceptions women are queens of their interior, and do not exercise this royal power in a very constitutional way. This led a Genoese man married to a creole woman to say, "One's opinion of this country could be what Machiavelli wrote about a Republican city in Italy: 'It's a paradise for women, a Purgatory for men, a hell for beasts.'"]

What Beck-Bernard is describing is a division of labor and responsibilities that grants women a space of power, of royalty inside the home. Women therefore have a space over which they have power within the family. In Beck-Bernard's case, this space is a humble building in a corner of Santa Fe, but the phrase "queens of their interior" might also extend to another "intériorité"—the Romantic idea of feelings and "vie intérieur." "Intérieur" takes two other meanings within the context of Beck-Bernard's text: the "interior" of the country as opposed to the coastal city of Buenos Aires, and the space of Romantic subjectivity. The notion of women as queens of their interior follows a mid-nineteenth-century ideology which looked upon the bourgeois woman as "the angel of the hearth," the absolute ruler of the bourgeois home and the possessor of a sensibility that made her adequate for this role. The word "intérieur" in the Argentina of the mid-1850s reverberated with images of the strife between Buenos Aires and the "interior," which violated the sacredness of feminine spaces and brought the violence of the battlefield into the domains of bourgeois women.

This reference to women's paradise is, however, deconstructed by Beck-Bernard herself in her chapter on the celebration of the anniversary of the May Revolution. Beck-Bernard describes the events of the day from the ringing of bells early in the morning to the disorganized presentation of arms by the national guard, cockfighting, and horse races. At night there is a ball at the Cabildo. Beck-Bernard arrives promptly at ten, the first person in the party, and observes as the room fills up not only with invited guests but also with gate-crashers, children, even dogs. The narrator sits next to Mercedes de L, the mother of one of the beautiful young debutantes. While Mercedes de L talks about the party, Beck-Bernard catches sight of what will become an aside in the narration yet is key to our understanding of the text:

Doña Mercedès me parlait de la fête lorsque, tout à coup, derrière son fauteuil et le mien, j'entends le vagissement d'un très-petite enfant; je me retourne vivement et je vois une Indienne qui avait son nourrisson enveloppé dans son châle et couché sur son épaule, selon la coutume des femmes du désert. Cette Indienne avait le teint bronzé, la figure triste, la

bouche entr'ouverte avec une sorte de dédain, les dents d'une blancheur
éclatante, la regard mélancolique, les cheveux incultes tombant tout droits
comme des crins; une couverture entortillée autour d'elle en guise de jupe,
la tête de son petit enfant paraissant au-dessus de son épaule, elle se tenait
droite et fière derrière le fauteuil de doña Mercedes, qui drapée dans une
magnifique robe de brocart, resplendissait sous ses dentelles de perles et de
brillants. C'était le luxe de la civilisation à côté de la barbarie, comme Santa-
Fé à côté du Chaco. Ces deux femmes personnifiaient, d'une manière
saisissante, deux races que trois cents années de luttes ont laissées ennemies
l'une vis-à-vis de l'autre, et qui resteront irréconciliables comme les peuples
dépossédés et les peuples envahissants le seront toujours. (*Le rio parana* 138)

[Doña Mercedes was talking to me about the party, when suddenly, from
behind her armchair and mine, I heard the cry of a very small child; turning
around, I saw an Indian woman who had her infant wrapped up in a blanket behind her back, as is the way of the women of the desert. This Indian
woman had tanned skin, a sad figure, the mouth half open with disdain,
the teeth of a dazzling whiteness, a melancholic gaze, unkempt hair falling
straight like a horse's, a blanket around her instead of a skirt, the face of her
small child coming out from behind her shoulders. She held herself straight
and strong behind the chair where doña Mercedes, dressed in a magnifi-
cent dress shone in her lace embroidered with pearls. It was the luxury of
civilization next to barbarism, like Santa Fe next to the Chaco. In a startling
way, these two women personified two races that three hundred years of
struggle have made into one another's enemies, and that will remain ir-
reconcilable, as dispossessed peoples and invading peoples will always be.]

Mercedes de L and the Indian woman are observers here but they are also observed by Beck-Bernard (who, after all, as a European writer, is there for the
show). These women make their way into Beck-Bernard's text as metaphors for
the most charged categories in Argentinean history: civilization and barbarism.
The Indian woman stands for the dispossessed (women and also gauchos and
Indians) who have no interior to reign over. Mercedes de L, on the other hand, has
two kingdoms: her own house and the open space of the streets and the plazas
where, as a symbol of the republic and its heroes, she can parade her royalty. The
women of Mercedes de L's social class—and probably Mercedes de L herself—
were creating other territories to rule over: charities, schools, hospitals for women
and children. The Indian woman, on the other hand, was being displaced and
excluded from all forms of interiority. She appears in the text, however, described
in detail in her role as mother, and as such in a comparable female role to that of
Mercedes de L and Beck-Bernard herself. Mercedes de L has produced a daugh-

ter for spectacle (she is one of the main attractions of the party); the Indian child (who has not been invited to the party) interrupts Mercedes de L's discussion of the party, reaffirms his/her presence, and captures the attention of the European onlooker. The Indian child interrupts, however momentarily, the narrative of the nation and its incipient rites.

Later on in the text, Beck-Bernard comes across "real Indians," Indians who had not yet been incorporated into "civilization" as the woman sitting next to Mercedes de L had. In a semi-destroyed house, Beck-Bernard sees a group of Indians, but she cannot make out their gender. After several changes of opinion, Beck-Bernard decides that in the group there are several men and one woman. Deprived of an interior to rule over, this Indian woman is also deprived of her femininity, and her gender is presented as ambiguous and unstable:

> Dans ce groupe il y a, en effet, *une femme;* mais nous ne la distinguons des hommes qu'à son jupon, fait d'une pièce d'étoffe entortillée autour d'elle; même costume, même physionomie, même taille, même mélancolie superbe, dans les gestes, les regards, l'attitude, comme tous les peuples destinés à mourir, et qui sentent instinctivement qu'ils assistent à l'agonie de leur race. (183)

> [In this group there is actually *a woman,* but we distinguish her from the men only by her skirt made from a piece of cloth wound around her— same clothing, same physiognomy, same size, same superb melancholy, in their gestures, their looks, their bearing, like all peoples who are destined to die out, and who instinctively feel that they are witnessing the death throes of their race.]

In *Le rio parana,* gauchos and native people are always connected to or represented by women. Beck-Bernard presents this uneasy and unstable situation of gender definition as chronologically preceding—and maybe leading to—disappearance. In the text, the gauchos are men and manly (even if they are introduced in connection with Manuelita Rosas); the "criollos" have taken on some of the characteristics of the gaucho and polished them with a European exterior. It is only the Indians who appear in a gender limbo included within the Romantic paradigm only as "noble savages." If we compare Lina Beck-Bernard's writings to her husband's, the contradictions become more apparent. Her husband's book *La république Argentine* extols the promise Argentina holds for immigrants and investors. Lina places Argentina in an isolated space within the context of the imperialist expansion of Europe. Considering the centrality of her family's role in the attempt to create a modern Argentina, Beck-Bernard's creation of a narrative space for the indigenous population is analogous to her creation of a narrative space for herself. The space she reigns over is her text; the space she assigns the dispossessed Indians to reign over is a small portion of her text, a discursive reservation.

Manuelita

The narrator of *Le rio parana* is a character in an unstable and ambiguous position. If Beck-Bernard as writer needed a role model for Beck-Bernard-the-narrator's ambiguous and unstable position, she found one in the country she was visiting. Manuelita functions as an axis around which Beck-Bernard structures her narration of Argentinean history and also her anthropological construction of the country. Manuelita is presented as a member of "civilization" living in—and reigning over—the stronghold of barbarism, and as such she is a European insider in the history of Buenos Aires and of the country. Beck-Bernard uses her as a tour guide of sorts, the European character through whose eyes we as readers try to make sense of recent Argentinean history. This is our introduction into the country and the unifying theme behind the Beck-Bernards' visit to Buenos Aires: once the Beck-Bernards get to Santa Fe, Beck-Bernard is on her own, and she shifts from a narrative style to a descriptive one. In Santa Fe, the space for her husband's colonizing schemes, Beck-Bernard produces static vignettes of a kind of life that was drastically altered once the northern European colonists arrived and the specific character and culture of the region was changed forever.

The portrait of Beck-Bernard in the Spanish version of her text bears a striking resemblance to the best-known portraits of Manuelita. For most Argentineans, Manuelita is the Manuelita portrayed by Pridiliano Pueyrredón: a young dark-haired woman dressed in red standing next to a desk, her hand resting on a piece of paper (a letter? a book?). Lina Beck-Bernard's portrait shows a similar dark-haired dark-eyed woman, her head similarly slanted to the left, her eyes looking straight ahead. In Beck-Bernard's case, the red federal attire is replaced by a white Romantic dress associated more with the melancholia she writes about than the resoluteness with which she writes and through which she most certainly braved the hardships of life in exile including the deaths of two of her children. Manuelita's portrait was made in the house she reigned over after the death of her mother (the ambiance in her portrait also reminds me of one of the most famous paintings of the time, *Boudoir Federal*). If the space of nineteenth-century middle-class women is the home, what better way to introduce a woman than in the context of the house she inhabits or once inhabited? Beck-Bernard first mentions Manuelita as an integral part of her own visit to Palermo. Beck-Bernard describes Palermo as the ghastly home of the dictator which is now in a state of decay since no one dares get too close to the site of so much recent suffering, but the house is "le souvenir d'une femme, de la bonne et gracieuse Manuelita, la fille de Rosas, [qui] adoucit, comme une ombre charmante, les légendes sinistres de Palermo" (83) [the memory of a woman, of the good and kindly Manuelita, the daughter of Rosas, who like a charming shadow, mitigates the sinister legends of Palermo]. Manuelita is presented as an innocent instrument of her father; she is the angel who made tyranny and dictatorship more endurable. Manuelita's moral survival in spite of her father's wrongdoings resonates with Josefina Ludmer's "tricks of the weak," which I discuss in the Introduction. Beck-Bernard's Manuelita shares with Beck-Bernard loyalty to a man who is erected as the authority but whose authority is minimized not by open rebellion but by small insubordinations that do not completely wear away at male authority but somehow erode it. Beck-Bernard shows Manuelita using her privileged space to affect the outcome of events (we see her intervening in favor of prisoners, persuading her father to grant a widow the right to give Christian burial to her husband). In her book, Beck-Bernard seems to be doing something similar to what she portrays Manuelita as doing: creating a space to reign over (in Beck-Bernard's case, her book). In this, like her Manuelita, she is not a passive observer but an agent, an underminer of patriarchal authority.

This subtle undermining is also present in Beck-Bernard's description of the gaucho. Beck-Bernard's first statement about the gaucho echoes those of the architects of national consolidation: "Le *gaucho* représente dans la confédération argentine l'élément rétrograde" (92) [In the Argentinean Confederation, the *gaucho* represents the reactionary element]. But her development of the description moves away from this kind of representation:

> Sa physionomie sauvage, mélancolique, est bronzée par le soleil et le vent des immenses pampas où il dompte ses chevaux et se laisse emporter par eux rapide comme la foudre, volant sur la pointe des herbes, dévorant l'espace, ne faisant qu'un avec l'animal fougueux sur lequel il saute d'un bond, une vraie incarnation moderne du centaure de la fable grecque. (93)

> [His savage, melancholy facial features are tanned by the sun and the wind of the wide pampas where he breaks his horses and lets them carry him away fast as lightning, flying on the tips of the grasses, devouring the spaces, being one with the spirited animal onto which he leaps with a bound, a true modern incarnation of the centaur of Greek mythology.]

This romantic description of the gaucho deviates from the stock description of the noble savage. For one thing, the gaucho is likened to a Greek centaur; his space is classical Greece—birthplace of Western of culture—instead of the stock barbarian sites such as Palestine. His sexuality, which is stressed in the image of the centaur, is toned down later in the description where he is defined as a "caballero" in the absolutely unambiguous sentence "il est caballero."

To appreciate the oxymoronic quality of this last sentence, I would like to contextualize my reading of the attitudes Beck-Bernard takes toward both Indians and gauchos. First of all, we must understand that for both European and creole writers of the time, the figure of the gaucho represents a composite of indigenous and white characteristics. The gaucho, universally defined as male, is the amalgamation of the qualities that created him as a type. In the paragraph quoted above, Beck-Bernard starts off with a list of the Indian-like characteristics of the gaucho—his savagery and his melancholy—and ends up with his most positive (white) characteristic—his resemblance to an element in a Greek (cultured, civilized) fable. In so doing, Beck-Bernard creates a glorious ancestry for the gaucho, but in displacing him to such a distant past she also exiles him from the modern Argentina her husband and his associates were creating.

In *Le rio parana,* it is possible to masquerade as someone else. Manuelita Rosas disguises herself as a gaucho but keeps her earrings as gender markers; Lina Beck-Bernard blends in in Santa Fe and can watch others without being watched. In the performance of nation, as in performances of gender, dress is paramount. A few months before the Beck-Bernards left Argentina, Urquiza was defeated by Mitre in the battle of Pavón. The unified nation was now ready to dramatize the dream of whiteness and homogeneity which the agricultural colonies of Santa Fe promised. In *Le rio parana,* this performance takes place in the context of a military parade. The soldiers from the provinces, Lina Beck-Bernard complains, "ont encore un aspect bizarre" (259) [still have a bizarre appearance]. Again, as in Mariquita Sánchez's description of British invasions, white Argentineans are charmed by European soldiers who know how to wear their uniforms. The European male soldier is presented as the model of desirability:

> Mais les soldats des provinces ont encore un aspect bizarre, peu fait pour plaire aux Européens. En voici un exemple: Un jeune sous-officier des chasseurs de Vicennes en sèmestre chez ses parent habitant la confédération argentine fut présenté au général ★★★, gouverneur de l'une des provinces. Le jeune sous-officier portait son uniforme avec la parfaite et gracieuse tenue qui caractérise nos soldats français. Le vieux général en fut charmé. "Restez avec moi, dit-il au jeune homme, je vous offre le grade de lieutenant-colonel dans mon état-major, avec 150 piastres de paye par mois." Le chasseur de Vincennes répondit sans hésiter et avec une franchise toute militaire: "Merci, mon général, j'apprécie votre offre; mais vous me permettrez de la refuser. J'aime mieux être sergent dans mon pays que lieutenant-colonel de le vôtre." (259)

[But the soldiers from the provinces still have a bizarre appearance that is unpleasing to Europeans. Here is an example of this: a young noncommissioned officer from the Vincennes regiment was on leave and staying with his parents who lived in the Argentinean Confederation; he was introduced to General ★★★, governor of one of the confederation's provinces. The young officer wore his uniform with the perfect and gracious posture which is characteristic of our French soldiers. The old general was charmed by it. "Stay with me," he said to the young man, "I offer you the rank of lieutenant-colonel in my staff, with 150 piastres per month in wages." The Vincennes infantryman answered without hesitating and with a thoroughly military straightforwardness, "Thanks you, General, I appreciate your offer, but permit me to refuse it. I prefer to be a sergeant in my own country than a lieutenant colonel in yours."]

The promise of a white Argentina which Charles Beck-Bernard championed and his wife, Lina, supported with mild enthusiasm is metaphorized in the inclusion (yet unfulfilled) of the desirable young Frenchman in the army—and the citizenship—of the nation. A promise mildly realized by the beginning of the twentieth century with a huge cost to all of those who could not successfully perform Europeanness.

2

Shifting Frontiers, 1880–1900

3

Eduarda Mansilla de García's
Recuerdos de Viaje: "Recordar es Vivir"[1]

. . . tenemos que mendigar al extranjero para tener más población, y sin
embargo, por otro lado, exterminamos a los de nuestra propia tierra. . . . Si
el territorio que han ocupado . . . siempre lo hemos considerado, en
nuestras cuestiones diplomáticas, como parte integrante del territorio de la
Nación, todos los allí nacidos . . . son ciudadanos argentinos por ese hecho.
Pero si se dice que el indio es extranjero, quiere decir que no ha nacido en
territorio argentino, luego ese territorio no debe pertenecernos.

[. . . we have to beg foreign nations in order to increase our population,
but on the other hand, we exterminate those of our own land. . . . If the
land that they have occupied . . . has always been considered by us, in
matters of diplomacy, as an integral part of the national territory, then all
those who were born there . . . are Argentinean citizens for that very reason.
But if it is said that the Indian is a foreigner, it means that he was not born
on Argentinean territory, and thus that land should not belong to us.]

Quoted by Barba, et al. 235–36

In one of the congressional debates that followed Argentina's expansion into
Patagonia, commonly known as the Campaign to the Desert, the future of the
inhabitants of the region had to be decided. The fact that one of the possibilities
which was seriously considered was declaring them foreigners says much about
the instability of the concept of nation and nationality in Argentina toward the
end of the nineteenth century. The same elite that was developing ways to

interpellate the white immigrants into allegiance to the nation was devising ways to disenfranchise the indigenous population. And superimposed on the white (male) citizenry and the indigenous "subhuman" population, the elites were articulating a discourse that likened the nation to the domestic order of landowning families: new immigrants could live, work, and prosper with the nation; only the selected families would rule. With the expansion to the south and the complete occupation of what Domingo Faustino Sarmiento had envisaged as the national territory, the dilemma of how to define and circumscribe the "nationals" became more problematic and more urgent. The Indians had been massacred and displaced, and the elites were to take their place as the owners of the land in both the literal and the metaphoric sense: through possession of the land, they had gained access to the creation of the land/nation.[2]

According to David Viñas, the accession of Julio Argentina Roca to the presidency marks the transformation of the Romantic nation imagined by Sarmiento and Juan Bautista Alberdi into a liberal state. This state inherits the models of colonization and land distribution that were so dear to Sarmiento and Alberdi. The 1880s is therefore the "classical moment of the Argentinean liberal élite" (*Indios, Ejércitos* 21) who will impose a paradigm of written legality which will organize work and land ownership. Indians will be excluded from this legality and so will gauchos inasmuch as they do not accept this new paradigm.

The debates surrounding the future of the Indians displaced from Patagonia and the creation of a modern nation with a modern capital city in Buenos Aires inform my discussion of Eduarda Mansilla's *Recuerdos de viaje. Recuerdos* was published twenty years after Mansilla's trip to the United States, but its subject matter is appropriate for Argentina of the 1880s. On the one hand, it delves into matters of race and nationality and specifically addresses the displacement of the U.S. native populations, while on the other hand it celebrates the advantages of life in a modern lay society such as the one the Argentinean positivists were striving to create.

When You Are Rosas's Niece . . .

In 1855, three years after Juan Manuel de Rosas was defeated in Caseros, his seventeen-year-old niece Eduarda Mansilla, who had once served as his translator, was the protagonist of a controversial love story described by the indefatigable Montevideo papers as an autochthonous version of Romeo and Juliet. Eduarda Mansilla—daughter of military hero General Lucio Mansilla and Rosas's sister Agustina—married Manuel García, the son of a staunch Rosas opponent and a diplomat for Justo José de Urquiza's government. This marriage realizes what Doris Sommer considers the necessary literary trope that throws "eros" and "polis" together (30–51). If we follow Sommer's argument, "national" novels in Latin America use love stories as metaphors of the need for national unification that would bring the principal elements of society together, like a family, united in love for the purposes of procreation. While the definition of nation was being actively and heatedly discussed in Argentina, this historical marriage brought together two families on opposing sides of the political sphere of the country and in their children the evidence of fruitful alliances.[3]

The trip to the United States narrated by Mansilla in her *Recuerdos de viaje* took place five years after her marriage to García. He and Mansilla had spent those five years in Paris, where García had a position in the Argentine embassy and where she was an active socialite. Mansilla, García, and their family traveled to the United States for the first time in 1860 on a diplomatic mission, and this is the trip which Mansilla narrates in her *Recuerdos de viaje*. With *Recuerdos,* Eduarda Mansilla de García inaugurates travel writing for Argentinean women. By the time her book was written and published, travel writing as a genre had a longstanding tradition in the country as a genre produced by males for whom the trip to Europe (and to a lesser extent to the United States) had an almost ritualistic meaning.[4] The trip to Europe had started off as a political tradition, first as the necessary exile from Rosas, then as the initiatory gesture of the elite men preparing for government abroad. In Eduarda Mansilla's case, the travelogue took on a different meaning: she was never in exile, and she would never govern. Her book, therefore, addresses areas only suggested in male travelogues: home, children, servants. Her book also bears witness to the fact that the pacification of the country allowed bourgeois women to enjoy the advantages of genteel life instead of forcing them into exile. The phrase *en touriste,* which both Eduarda and her brother Lucio V. Mansilla use repeatedly in their writings, is symptomatic of the new spirit of this period. Mansilla's language in *Recuerdos* is saturated with English words that remind the reader that above all this is a travel guide. These words—"confort" [*sic*], "home," "laundry," "waiter" —always appear in italics and are seldom translated into Spanish. This language of tourism and leisure is adequate for the image the protagonist of *Recuerdos* creates of herself: a modern woman, at ease in ships, buses, and hotels. Mansilla's *Recuerdos* more than any other of her works anticipates María Rosa Oliver's and Victoria Ocampo's writings on leisure travel abroad.[5] Travel and tourism became another subject for women of the upper class to explore in novels, memoirs, short stories, and journalistic essays. By the beginning of the twentieth century, most women writers of the upper class devoted large parts of their works to vacations, vacation spots, travels abroad, and the reiterated retirement to the "estancia."[6]

Recuerdos de viaje narrates Mansilla's stay in the United States during the Civil War while her husband was commissioned to study the justice system in the Argentine embassy in Washington, D.C. In both his diplomatic missions to the United States, García worked under the supervision of Sarmiento, whose *Viajes* also includes a narrative of his trip to the United States. *Recuerdos* starts with Mansilla on her way to New York with her husband and children and finishes with her leaving New York to return to Europe for a new diplomatic assignment. Her stay in the United States lasts four years, but Mansilla never mentions specific dates, and even though she lived in Washington for a few years she does not delve into the mundane details of daily life in the city. Mansilla describes New York, Washington, D.C., Philadelphia, Niagara Falls and parts of southeast Canada, Staten Island, and Boston, and she mentions other cities such as Baltimore in passing. In her description of Washington, she does include vignettes of Washington nightlife: the social life among diplomats and U.S. politicians. *Recuerdos de viaje* is written as a guide for Argentineans traveling to the United States. There are practical references to what kind of lodging and restaurants to choose and which sights to visit. Throughout the book, Mansilla also includes her own reflections on modernization and on race and gender relations. Two readers are directly mentioned in the book: Barbosa, a physician who in Mansilla's words "me ha impulsado a escribir mis *Recuerdos de viaje*" [has propelled me to write my *Travel Memories*], and Santiago Arcos. Arcos, an author of books on the indigenous populations of South America, is also Lucio V. Mansilla's interlocutor in *Una excursión a los indios ranqueles*. Arcos is described by both Mansillas as an enlightened man of the future, a compendium of the good elements of liberalism. For Eduarda Mansilla, he is also a father figure who puts aesthetic values in the context of philosophical and ethical ones. The wider readership that Mansilla expected for her travelogue is the Argentinean elite whom Mansilla never directly addresses but whom she includes in her adjective "nuestro/a," which she uses throughout her text. In *Recuerdos* more than in any other of her works, it is possible to infer what being Argentinean meant for Mansilla. The identity in flux which I mentioned at the beginning of this section is articulated throughout Mansilla's works. She is probably the first Argentinean woman writer for whom a definition of identity as an Argentinean rather than as a "unitaria," "federal," or the by-then anachronistic "americana" is essential. In seeing herself as an Argentinean, she could renounce the conflictive past which for her was also the history of her own family.[7] The adjective "argentino/a" is never used; the possessive adjective "nuestro" is used in its place, and Argentina is never mentioned except as "la patria ausente" (193) [the absent native land] or ironically as "una República de nada" (93) [a republic of nothing].

The preoccupation with "lo nuestro" appears in most of Mansilla's works as well as in those of her male cohorts. It is explicitly articulated in Mansilla's introduction to a collection of children's stories she published in Buenos Aires the same year she published *Recuerdos:*

> La acogida benévola que obtuvo Chinbrú, publicado en folletín, acentuó en mí la idea que desde Europa me atormentaba tiempo há, cuando mis hijitos que adoran á Andersen, devoraban ávidos las obras de la Condesa de Ségur, tan popular en Francia. Casi con envidia veía el entusiasmo con que esas inteligencias, esos corazones que eran míos, asimilaban sentimientos é ideas que yo no les sugería; y más de una vez traté de cautivar á mi turno con mis narraciones, al grupo infantil. (*Cuentos* vii)

> [The kind reception that Chinbrú received, published as a newspaper serial, impressed upon me the idea that had been tormenting me since Europe, when my children, who love Andersen, avidly devoured the works of the Countess de Ségur, so popular in France. Almost with envy, I would see the enthusiasm with which those sharp minds, my very own dears, assimilated feelings and ideas that were not my own; and more than once I had tried to captivate the children with my own narrations.]

Mansilla's children's stories in the collection include mostly cosmopolitan themes with a few incursions to American themes such as references to the May Revolution and to American plants and animals. To infer what Mansilla considers factors that define "nuestro" from the disparate elements of the stories would be very hard indeed. In her *Recuerdos,* the elements that circumscribe "lo nuestro" appear in a somewhat clearer way: "lo nuestro," which is what Mansilla as travel writer and her readers share, includes two languages (Spanish and French), a religion (Catholicism), and a way of life which mirrors the life of the upper class in France.

In her "Preliminares" (Preliminaries) to *Recuerdos,* Mansilla makes her allegiances clear when, after an extended discussion on the differences between British and French ships, she says:

> Y aquí, para no ser ingrata ni olvidadiza con una nación que tanto quiero, diré, que personalmente, yo prefiero hasta naufragar con los Franceses. (12)

> [And here, so as not to be ungrateful to nor forgetful with a nation that I love so much, I will say, that personally, I would even prefer to be shipwrecked with the French.]

France, the French, and Paris are the standards against which everything is measured. France and French as a language are not presented as foreign for the narrator and her readers. "Anglo-Saxon" is presented in opposition to "lo nuestro," whereas French is highlighted as the most desirable element of "lo nuestro." French is learned without effort, as a mother tongue; English, on the other hand, has to be learned, requires effort, and never comes naturally to the narrator. For Mansilla, Argentina is closer to France than to the United States, but the United States and Argentina share the characteristic of being "American."[8] The American elements in the culture are introduced in the context of their newness or youth in comparison to the centuries-old culture of the European capitals (she mentions Madrid, London, Vienna, and, of course, Paris). "Americanness" is also depicted as an exotic element, a spectacle:

> El cosmopolitismo hállase más acentuado en Nueva York; pero la raza sajona descuella allí sobre las demás é imprime a la metrópoli norte americana, todo el carácter de una ciudad inglesa. Si se exceptuan los "tobacconish," con sus colosales cigarros de madera chocolate ó sus indias de lo mismo, adornadas con el clásico tocado y la cintura de plumas rojas y azules que tienen un sello puramente americano. (23)

> [Cosmopolitanism is found more pronounced in New York; but the Saxon race stands out among the rest and imprints all the features of an English city on the North American metropolis. If one is to leave out the "tobacconish," with their colossal chocolate-brown wooden cigars or their similarly constructed Indian women, decorated with the classic headdress and the red and blue feathered waistbands that have a purely American hallmark.]

The reference to Indians, as in the above passage, and the reference to feathers, in particular, appear repeatedly throughout the book. Mansilla shows herself empathetic with the plight of the U.S. Indians:

> Dolorosa es la historia, que llamaré privada, de los Estados Unidos, en contacto con esas tribus salvajes, que poblaban los territorios de Nevada, Colorado, etc. Así que el Yankee tuvo una existencia política asegurada, no se contentó ya con comprar, como en otro tiempo tierras a los indígenas, decidió destruir la raza por todos los medios a su alcance. Muerte, traición y rapiña, han sido las armas con las cuales los han combatido; promesas y engaños, hé ahí su política con los hijos del desierto. (53–54)

> [Painful is the story, which I shall call private, of the United States' contact with those savage tribes that populated the territories of Nevada, Colorado, etc. In this way the Yankee had an assured political existence. He did not content himself with simply buying the land from the indigenous people,

as he had in other times. He decided to destroy the race through any means at his disposal. Death, treason, and robbery have been the weapons with which they have fought them. Promises and deceit, such is the politics against the children of the desert.]

Mansilla's denunciation of the Indian genocide is situated in the context of the white legend of the colonization of the Americas. For her, the root of the mistreatment of the Indians by the U.S. government has to be looked for in the racial background of the inhabitants of the United States, since, for her, this cruelty shows "una similitud notable, que encuentro entre el Sajón de Europa y el trasplantado al Nuevo Mundo" (53) [a notable similarity that I find between the European Saxon and the New World transplant]. She even quotes the *London Times* to further support this theory. Her impassioned defense of the Indians whom she calls "children of the desert," a phrase commonly used in connection with Argentinean Indians, ends in solidarity and admiration for the "dueños de la tierra" (55) [owners of the land]. I believe her condemnation of genocide is focused on the U.S. situation, but the United States functions as a reflection of Argentinean political and social concerns. We must remember that 1880 marks the accession to the Argentine presidency of Julio Argentino Roca, the general in charge of the annihilation of the Argentine native populations of Patagonia, and Mansilla's use of the term "children of the desert" had unequivocal connotations for Argentinean readers of the time.

Although sympathetic to the plight of the Native Americans, Mansilla is completely myopic to the suffering of blacks. She admits to having supported the South in the American Civil War, and she defines the South as "simpático" and elegant and bemoans the fact that the genteel life of the South had necessarily to end with the abolition of slavery. Support of slavery is justified in the context of elegance and good manners:

En el comienzo de la guerra, la alta sociedad filadelfiana, era casi toda sudista; y aquellos que no tenían en realidad opinión decidida, no perdían ocasión, sin embargo, de decir a los extranjeros: *Oh! Sólo en el Sud existe la verdadera elegancia.* Parecía este dicho ser como un exponente de buen gusto, de refinamiento, y quizá lo era: es decir que la moda consistía entonces, para los elegantes, en ser sudistas, ó si se quiere, que los sudistas, habiendo hasta entonces, empuñado el cetro de la elegancia, no lo habían cedido aún, a esas nuevas capas sociales, que surgieron más tarde con su ruina. (108)

[At the beginning of the war, Philadelphia's high society was almost completely pro-South; and those who did not really have a fixed opinion did not lose any opportunity to tell foreigners: *Oh! Only in the South can you find true elegance.* This saying seemed to be like an expression of good taste, of refinement, and perhaps it was. That is to say that for the elegant, fashion then consisted of being Southern. Or, if you wish, that the Southerners, having wielded until then the scepter of elegance, had not yet given it up to those new social strata that later arose from the South's deterioration.]

Throughout the book, Mansilla trivializes slavery, using adjectives such as "simpático" [charming], "elegante" [elegant], "refinado" [refined], and "monopolizador de la cultura" [monopolizer of culture] to refer to the order of the South. Slavery is presented in the context of genteel life for women of the middle classes, and even though Mansilla praises republicanism as an egalitarian system, she is nostalgic for the advantages older monarchic societies offer the affluent:

El oficio de sirviente, es más complicado de lo que en las Américas se cree, y tanto nosotros como los Yankees estamos servidos por *aficionados.* (123)

[The job of servant is more complex than what is believed in the Americas. We, as much as the Yankees, are being served by *amateurs.*]

In her use of "nosotros," the first person plural, Mansilla includes members of her own social class who in Argentina also stand for the old order. In her short fiction set in Argentina, Mansilla contrasts the faithful service of blacks and mestizos with the unreliability of the new immigrant Italian and Spanish servants. For Mansilla, manual labor is undignified for women of her social class whom she includes among the "nosotros." Thus her dramatization of the downfall of slavery shows the debacle of upper-class women:

Cayó vencido, aniquilado ese Sud tan simpático a pesar de sus errores; y sus mujeres más hermosas, más educadas, más opulentas, tuvieron que vivir del trabajo de sus manos. Algunas damas de la mejor sociedad, de Nueva Orleans, se vieron reducidas á ser hasta cocineras. ¡Expiación horrenda! ¡Lección cruel, que llegó a enterner a esos mismos esclavos, libertados por las llamas y el hierro del vencedor! (196)

[Conquered and annihilated, that kind South fell, despite its errors. Its most beautiful, educated, and opulent women had to live off the labor of their own hands. Some ladies of the best society, from New Orleans, even saw themselves reduced to cooks. Horrendous atonement! A cruel lesson that came to move those same slaves, freed by the flames and iron of the victor.]

In this passage, the next to final paragraph of *Recuerdos,* Mansilla performs a move that brings together her preoccupations with race and gender. Social reform is depicted as threatening the social position of middle-class women. We must remember that between her trip to the United States in the 1860s and the writing of this travelogue in the 1870s, the Paris Commune and the installation of the Third Republic had taken place in France.[9] Mansilla's insistence on the advantages of monarchy has to be read in this historical context. Mansilla is evidently a believer in a strict social hierarchy that supersedes national and religious identities. Her discussions of Catholicism in the United States, therefore, are not very substantial and are immersed in the context of another discussion of servants:

> Quizá, con ese espíritu práctico, eminentemente utilitario de los Americanos, la dama protestante se hacía este raciocinio, en extremo correcto: Siendo católica, mi sirvienta no tendrá inconveniente en servirme el Domingo, y de esa suerte podré utilizarla como los demás días de la semana. (132–33)

> [Perhaps with that practical, eminently utilitarian mind of Americans, the Protestant lady would, quite rightly, reason thus: Being a Catholic, my servant will not mind serving me on Sundays, and with this good fortune I will be able to use her like the other days of the week.]

Unlike later travel writers such as Delfina Bunge for whom religion is an important issue (and who would most probably be horrified by the above passage), Mansilla does not believe that Catholicism deserves major attention. When she describes Protestant churches, she is critical more on aesthetic than on moral terms. She admires the religious tolerance (even including tolerance of Judaism) that is *de rigueur* among the generation of 1880 but which will be fiercely criticized by the Argentine Catholic nationalists at the beginning of the twentieth century.

Mansilla's concerns about race, slavery, and servitude are present in most of her works. Livery as a mark of social class and indenture is often given preeminence in her European stories where the servants are absolutely identified with the masters and faithful to them.[10] In *Recuerdos,* Mansilla includes a telling anecdote:

> No puedo prescindir de recordar aquí la respuesta que me dio algunos años después, un Virginiano, cochero, a quien exigía se pusiera la librea con los colores de la República Argentina: "Señora," me dijo, "yo sé bien que eso no deshonra a nadie; pero soy tan joven . . . y quién sabe si llego algún día a ser Presidente . . . pueden reprochármelo." "Tiene Ud., razón, John," le contesté; y tomé un negro. (125)

[I cannot go without remembering here the answer given to me a few years later by a Virginian driver, when I requested that his livery be decorated with the colors of the Argentine republic: "Ma'am," he told me, "I know well that this does not dishonor anyone; but I am so young . . . and who knows if one day I manage to be president . . . they could turn it against me." "You are right, John," I answered him; and I hired a black man.]

Mansilla's presentation of herself here is similar to her description of Parisian ladies in her European short stories. Throughout *Recuerdos,* Mansilla complains about the quality of service and servants in the United States, where what she calls the "democratic spirit" interferes by instilling ideas of equality in subalterns. In the above passage, we are privy to her perceptions of blacks as outside this realm of equality. Her inclusion of this anecdote in her travelogue attests to Mansilla's complete unawareness of her own racism.

Mansilla's belief in a hierarchical social system is further manifested in her discussion of white North American women's place in society:[11]

La mujer en la Unión Americana, es soberana absoluta; el hombre vive, trabaja y se eleva por ella y para ella. Es ahí que debe buscarse y estudiarse la influencia femenina y no en sueños de emancipación política. ¿Qué ganarían las Americanas con emanciparse? Más bien perderían, y bien lo saben. (114)

[The woman of the American Union is an absolute sovereign; the man lives, works and is exalted by her and for her. It is there that one must find and study the feminine influence and not in dreams of political emancipation. What would American women gain by emancipation? They would lose, and they know it.]

This image of the sovereignty of women is very telling and is shared by other travel writers such as Lina Beck-Bernard. Paradoxically enough, Beck-Bernard uses it to describe Argentinean women for a French-reading public, and Mansilla uses it to describe North American women to her Argentine readers. However, Beck-Bernard describes Argentine women's power inside the home, whereas Mansilla extends women's power to the public space: "[l]as mujeres influyen en la cosa pública por medios que llamaré psicológicos e indirectos" (114) [women have influence in the public sphere by means that I shall call psychological and indirect]. Mansilla endorses indirect participation by women in public life but condemns emancipation. However, she uses the word "emancipación" in a positive context a few paragraphs later:

Reporters femeninos, son los que describen con amor el color de los trajes de las damas, su corte, sus bellezas, sus misterios, sus defectos; y a fe que lo hacen concienzuda y científicamente. Los Yankees desdeñan, y con razón ese reportismo que tiene por tema encajes y sedas; hallan sin duda la tarea poco varonil. Es una lástima que en los demás países no suceda otro tanto. En ello además, las mujeres tienen un medio honrado intelectual para ganar su vida: y se emancipan así de la cruel servidumbre de la aguja, servidumbre terrible desde la invención de las máquinas de coser. (115)

[Women reporters are those who describe with love the color of ladies' suits, their tailoring, their beauty, their mystery, their defects; and you can be assured they do it conscientiously and scientifically. Rightly so, the Yankees disdain that type of reporting that concerns itself with lace and silk; without a doubt, they consider the task not manly enough. It is a shame that in other countries this does not occur more frequently. There, women have an honored intellectual milieu in which to earn a living: and they emancipate themselves from the cruel servitude of the needle; a terrible servitude from the invention of the sewing machine.]

For Mansilla, emancipation for middle-class women translates into intellectual work circumscribed by "feminine concerns," especially journalism. "Servidumbre" is a negative word in the passage above, yet throughout most of her book it has a positive connotation for those who are served, who use servants to make their lives easier and more pleasant. Any emancipation which includes political reform, be it for women or for blacks, is suspect for Mansilla. Birth control and abortion are presented in her travelogue as aberrations, and it is not surprising that Mansilla prudishly refuses to even deal with those subjects and refers her readers to a book by an obstetrician in case they are interested in the subject:

Como a mí me repugna por demás, tratar esta cuestión, de una importancia vital, empero, para todas las sociedades, recomiendo al lector, que guste de profundizarla, las obras del Dr. T. Gaillard Thomas, célebre Profesor de Nueva York, especialista de obstetricia, sumamente interiorizado en las costumbres de la sociedad Yankee. Yo prefiero pasearme tranquilamente por la Quinta Avenida, esa espléndida calle de mansiones de mármol blanco, que parece pertenecer a ciudades de las Mil y una noche. (138)

[Since I abhor dealing with that question of vital importance for all societies, I recommend, for the reader who is interested in examining the matter further, the works of Dr. T. Gaillard Thomas, celebrated New York professor of obstetrics, who is extremely well versed in the customs of Yankee society. I, on the other hand, prefer to stroll quietly down Fifth Avenue, that splendid street of white marbled mansions that appears to belong to the cities of Thousand and One Nights.]

Maybe this last statement most aptly expresses Mansilla's ideology in *Recuerdos*. Her escape from the problems that she herself considers "de una importancia vital" [of vital importance] to a fantasy land of luxury defined by the whiteness and the coldness of marble is symptomatic of her attitude as a travel writer. Mansilla's travelogue is seductive because of its readability, its casual and light tone, its light-heartedness. Underneath its superficial charm, there is, however, a complex structure that draws its input from the most reactionary discourses available at the time, which naturalize power, discrimination, racism, and xenophobia. That this combination of charm and acute intolerance of difference is present in many, if not most, travel books still being produced today must serve as a cautionary note for all of us.

4

Interlude in the Frontier:
Lady Florence Dixie's *Across Patagonia*

Throughout the nineteenth century, Argentinean writers drew on European travelers to create their own versions of what Argentina was and what it should become. The British gaze, rewritten in Spanish by creole writers, worked as an unreliable but relied-upon mirror of Argentine reality and as a crucial element in the creation of a national project for the literate elites. By the time of the Campaign to the Desert in 1879–80, Argentina had been "put on the maps," as it were, by numerous accounts in European and American magazines, travel journals, and travel books. The existence of a government which looked favorably on foreign investment was a further incentive for all sorts of traveling entrepreneurs: miners, businessmen, investors, cattle-ranchers. The availability of land and economic possibilities whereby a male European of average intelligence could become rich overnight were sufficient encouragement for visitors and offered ample opportunity for later reports—to the institution that had paid for the trip, to the employer, to family, to "posterity." Men retold the outcome of their visit: becoming rich, exploring economic possibilities. The question most travel writers sought to answer was: "Could an average European become rich here?" The answer most of them gave was "yes."

Not many travelogues by women on Argentina were published in this period. One of the reasons might be that most travel literature on Argentina published during the period had a more practical goal; travel books which would open up South America to capitalist exploits were traditionally written by men. Most travelogues by European women during the period were concerned with the "Orient" (North Africa for Frenchwomen, India for their

British counterparts) or with Africa. Florence Dixie, the author I discuss in this chapter, gained notoriety in literary circles in Britain with her travelogues on South Africa and her impassioned defense of the Zulus. Before she ventured into South Africa, she had traveled to Patagonia, a region which figured prominently in British travel writing thanks mainly to the works of Charles Darwin and Thomas Graham. Unlike those authors, Dixie was not an explorer, a scientist, or a businesswoman. She was a tourist, looking for leisure and a good time.

Dinnertime in Patagonia

> But whatever country one is in, whatever scenes one may be among—in one's own cosy snuggery in England, or in the bleak steppes of Patagonia—there is a peculiar sameness in the feeling that comes over one towards the hours of evening, and which inevitably calls up the thought, It must be getting near dinner-time.
>
> *Across Patagonia*

"Una lady viajó a la Patagonia . . ." Thus began an article published in *La Bandera Liberal* in Argentina in 1881, two years after the end of the Campaign to the Desert and a year after Lady Florence Dixie's trip to Patagonia. Twenty-three at the time, Dixie was a British aristocrat who traveled to Patagonia to escape the boredom of her life in London. The trip is a leisure one during which her political sensibilities are aroused by the native population only inasmuch as they compare favorably to Victorian habits. The quotation above is significant: what Dixie points out is a sameness in Patagonia and England which refers back to herself. In her writing, everything refers back to Dixie as protagonist, as seeing eye, as experiencer.

Born in 1857, raised partly in England and partly in France, Dixie married in 1875 when she was already a published poet. Her *Across Patagonia,* published in New York in 1881, provides an interesting ground of comparison for hegemonic discourses in travel narratives at the time. With its title page illustration of a dog Dixie took back to Britain with her and with the book's humble dedication to the Prince of Wales (without the by-then characteristic allusion to the economic prospects of the region), Dixie's narrative of her "wanderings over unexplored and untrodden ground" is, from the outset, anomalous.

I want to echo Inderpal Grewal's statement: "I take it as a given that various imperial, racist, and gendered narratives were art of the lives of all women who lived in England, and that these affected participation in Victorian imperial culture" (9). I therefore want to argue that Dixie's participation in the genre of travel writing in general and in the writing of Patagonia in particular is of course marked by these imperial, racist, and gendered narratives while it resists others. By reading Dixie's text, I intend to highlight the existence of discourses other than the hegemonic male discourse of conquest, plunder, and extinction. I want to suggest that during the nineteenth century, there were other possibilities to hegemonic discourses. Dixie's writing on Patagonia challenges the tradition of writing on the region started by Darwin. Male travel writers refer to each other, quote each other, and share each other's basic assumptions on the region. By neglecting to quote any of these figures, Dixie disclaims their authority and challenges their hegemonic position. My reading of *Across Patagonia* investigates the ways in which Dixie both appropriates and challenges the conventions of this tradition. The actual physical location of her writing is the frontier, not defined in her text as a place of danger but rather as a paradisiacal locale where gender relations are fruitful and harmonic.

Imaginary spaces in the colonial era often correspond to erotic male fantasies—penetration, rape, availability of native women. The imperial scheme is metaphorized as an act of penetration and subjugation; whole populations are feminized, their bodies read and written on. The vocabulary used by men in the central tradition of travel writing is difficult for women to appropriate. In this discourse, women are metaphors and objects, not speaking subjects. Travel writers on Patagonia had always feminized the region, stressing its vacuity, its infertility. Within the tradition of male travel writing on Patagonia, the region was represented as an empty and barren woman ready to be penetrated and fertilized, a conflation of all women, both virginal and treacherous at once. It is in a tone, borrowed from this central tradition of travel narrative, that Dixie sets out after explaining that her voyage was instigated by a disgust with "the artificiality of modern experience" combined with the advantage of Patagonia being a region where she can be

> safe from the persecutions of fevers, friends, savage tribes, obnoxious animals, telegrams, letters, and every other nuisance you are elsewhere liable to be exposed to. To these attractions was added the thought, always alluring to an active mind, that there too *I should be able to penetrate into vast wilds, virgin* as yet to the foot of man. Scenes of infinite beauty and grandeur might be lying hidden in the silent solitude of the mountains which bound the barren plains of the Pampas, into whose mysterious recesses no one as yet had ever ventured. And *I was the first to behold them?*—an egotistical pleasure, it is true; but the idea had a great charm for me, as it had for many others. (3)

If the Western gaze has been theorized as male, few discourses provide more examples of the determinacy of the male gaze than travel narratives. In these narratives, the gaze is not only male but white and European too. According to

Figure 3. Julius Beerbohm, "An Indian Camp." In Julius Beerbohm, *Wanderings in Patagonia*.

Raymond Williams, any description of landscape or scenery is constructed by the axis of the viewing eye and what is viewed. Travel narratives in the late nineteenth century erase the viewing eye from the description. The description employs elements that are supposed to make it objective and therefore generalizable and usable for scientific and/or mercantilistic purposes. Dixie's narratives subvert these conventions of the objective male gaze by localizing the gaze before the description of what is gazed at and by making the two most privileged objects of the gaze—natives and women—subjects.

The illustrations in Dixie's book are excellent examples of this "subjectivity of the gaze." The illustrator, Julius Beerbohm, is introduced by Dixie as a member of her group. His book, *Wanderings in Patagonia*, had just come out when they started their excursion. The second edition of *Wanderings in Patagonia* was published in 1881 in London while Dixie's *Across Patagonia* was being published in New York. The difference between the illustrations Beerbohm publishes in his own book and those in Dixie's book is paradigmatic of larger differences at other narrative levels. The most interesting contrast is that between the two depictions of an "Indian camp." Beerbohm's Indian camp (figure 3) is the stock portrayal of the time. The Indians seem to be unaware of the looking eye describing them (none of them is actually facing the viewer of the picture), and

Figure 4. Julius Beerbohm, "Indian Camp." In Florence Dixie, *Across Patagonia*.

they are all overengaged in activities.[1] The excess of simultaneous activities on the part of the Indians seems to be hinting at the picture's function as a summa of Indian life, even at the expense of credibility or verisimilitude. In the illustration in Dixie's book (figure 4), on the contrary, the main and only event is the arrival of the foreigner.[2] This arrival marks the disruption of daily activities. The eye-lines of the Indian are concentrated on Dixie and the members of her travel party. The main focus of the picture, however, is the woman on the right who is holding a baby and is looking straight at *us* (readers, voyeurs, onlookers). Eyes are privileged parts in the spatial delineation of the imperial subject. Eyesight grants credibility and authority. The traveler retains the privilege of the gaze and of intelligent sight and reserves for the Indian eyes that are either empty or laden with passion (as opposed to the intelligence of the Europeans' eyes). In graphic depictions—photographs and sketches—the Indians' eyes are always blurred or looking elsewhere.

Why is this Indian woman looking at us? She is not only defying the rule that the native does not look back, but she is also looking back with interest and curiosity—attributes of the European male. What this woman in Beerbohm's sketch in Dixie's book gives us is a portrait of "human curiosity" that reciprocates the "human curiosity" Dixie and her team possess. There are other interesting elements in the picture: the woman is placed in the typical mother-child dyad position codified in Western art. Furthermore, there are two small children looking at her, while she looks out of the picture at us, somehow protecting and representing the whole family in the looking and the being looked at. The representation of the Indian woman as mother in the timeless madonna-like dyad is quite exceptional in the iconography of the period, and it breaks the dichotomy between "good" and "bad" women. In this picture, the native woman—generally associated with lust and passion—is placed in the most privileged space Western discourse has reserved for women. In Beerbohm's sketch in his own book, on the other hand, the European is absent and the picture attempts to depict the "other" as an "exoticized" sight. The artificiality of the scene/seen comes clear when the viewer tries to codify the multiplicity of activities going on at the same time. The fact that someone had to put together the picture ex post facto—and that this is a montage prepared for the British onlooker—is evident.[3] There is an overwhelming simultaneity of occupations more appropriate to industrial London than to Patagonia, especially since, except for a few examples (the man using the "boleadoras" on the near right, the young man next to him running aimlessly, the man at the back inexplicably galloping behind the horses), what Beerbohm represents are various forms of indolence, which he attributes to the Indians. Interpersonal relations in the picture happen only in pairs, and the Indians who in the narrative description are collectivized and defined in terms of community traits suffer here from a strange reifying syndrome. The lack of connection and lack of unity of the Indian community remind us of the words commonly used to describe Indian languages: "grunt," "guttural," "disgruntled." What is portrayed here is definitely a microcosm of inarticulate beings who are not communicating with each other. The readers of the day would possibly relate the lack of purpose in the Indians' activities and their loitering as both symptom and cause of their imminent disappearance. James Clifford describes this technique of "'pastoral' encodation" as "a relentless placement of others in a present becoming past. . . . 'Primitive,' nonliterate, underdeveloped, tribal societies are constantly yielding to progress, 'losing' their traditions" (*Writing* 114–15).

A remarkable characteristic of Dixie's writing and one that sets her apart from others is that whenever she writes herself as viewer, she herself is also looked at, viewed, defined. Her first encounter with a "real Patagonian Indian" is marked by mutual gazes and by Indians and Europeans being all on horseback, and thus at the same physical level:

> We reined in our horses when he got close to us, to have a good look at
> him, and he doing the same, for a few minutes we stared at him to our

hearts' content, receiving in return as minute and careful a scrutiny from him. Whatever he may have thought of us, we thought him a singularly unprepossessing object, and, for the sake of his race, we hoped an unfavorable specimen of it. (63)

This description is characteristic of Dixie's writing in several ways, the most outstanding of which is the combination of a reactionary discourse of otherness that privileges a racial purity ("real Patagonian Indian," insistence on pure-breed Indians) and draws deprecatory descriptions, together with a transgressive acknowledgment of mutual difference and of reciprocity, where the European also becomes the "object of the gaze." Likewise in the picture there is an awful lot of "looking" going on, the most notable examples being the woman on the right looking out of the picture and the exchange of looks between the Indian (I have difficulty deciding whether the drawing means to depict a man or a woman) and Dixie. Of course, something has to be made of the difference between Dixie looking down from the horse and the Indian character having to look up, but the mutual look itself is significant mainly because it is usually conspicuously absent from the genre, and because it includes the narrator/viewer as much as the narrated/viewed.[4] The chapter in Dixie's book that describes the visit to the Indian camp, both verbally and by means of the sketch I have already mentioned, is striking in its departure from the conventions of travel writing. The first "real Patagonian Indian" rides away, and the Europeans are again observed—this time by several mounted Indians on the top of a ridge—before they can look back. It is only after these two encounters that Dixie gets to the trope of the arrival scene: the Indians watching in "lazy curiosity," the Europeans responding in "leisurely observation"; the distribution of sugar among the Indian children; the exchange of sugar for meat; the Indians' examination of Dixie's boots and bracelets; the mutual inspection. Dixie also interpolates physical descriptions of the Indians and comparisons between what she expected them to be like and what she thought of them on meeting them.

Interestingly enough, Dixie does not acknowledge any sources for her way of reading and of looking at the Patagonian Indians. This absence is especially remarkable since an acknowledgment of being well versed in previous narrations of the region and an ongoing dialogue with previous travelers was a well-established characteristic of the genre. Dixie only quotes Beerbohm. Beerbohm, on the other hand, refers to the canonized narrators of Patagonia such as Musters and Darwin. In spite of this absence of source citations, Dixie shows from the outset that she is acquainted with the mythical representations of the region, and her text can be quite insightfully read against and next to Beerbohm's. Beerbohm's *Wanderings in Patagonia* is the only book Dixie mentions. While Beerbohm was a co-traveler in her expedition, his outlook differs greatly from Dixie's. Beerbohm is an engineer on a surveying excursion; Dixie, on the other hand, is an aristocrat "palled for the moment with civilization and its surroundings," who goes on this trip to escape the "shallow artificiality of modern existence" (2). Dixie's book is fascinating in its interweaving of hegemonic and non-hegemonic discourses. For example, her attitude toward the English servant class is absolutely deprecatory, as one would expect from an aristocratic woman:

> We only took one servant with us, knowing that English servants inevitably prove a nuisance and hindrance in expeditions of the kind, when a great deal of "roughing it" has to be gone through, as they have an unpleasant knack of falling ill at inopportune moments. (3–4)

Yet, at the same time, Dixie does not indulge in the idealization or the infantilization of the Indians that characterizes the work of most other writers of her time. She devotes more narrative space to the women than to the men. Furthermore, her description of Indian women is radically different from—and far more sympathetic than—any other written at the time.

The way Dixie interweaves narrative with general information on the Indians is unique. Her generalizations are always subordinated to the narrative, and her use of the "ethnographic present" (in Johannes Fabian's terms) is devoted to areas which were usually absent from men's travel narratives (marriage, relationships between spouses, child care). Undoubtedly Dixie obtained much of the background information from Beerbohm, but in reworking this information, her interpretation differs strongly from his. Although her writing unveils the relationship between seeing eye, description, and interpretation, Dixie chooses not to mention her sources of information that challenge the prevalent views. Another way of looking at this chapter is to consider it an example of a woman writing in the margins: instead of encroaching in "male" topics and writing about means of production and economic organization of the Indians (with a helpful hint to readers that these Indians could be used as sources of information or cheap labor), she dwells on information that is "feminine" (it deals with home and family, it has no "practical application"). In her portrayal of the Tehuelche Indians, she includes characteristics which male writers had denied Patagonian Indian women (industriousness, beauty, capacity to nurture, conjugal happiness), and by so doing she implicitly compares conditions for women in Britain with conditions among more "primitive" groups.[5]

> But it is only men who are cursed or blessed with this indolent spirit. The women are indefatigably industrious. All the work of Tehuelche existence

is done by them except hunting. When not employed in ordinary house-hold work they busy themselves in making guanaco capas, weaving gay-coloured garters and fillets for the hair, working silver ornaments, and so forth. Not one of their least arduous tasks is that of collecting firewood, which, always a scarce article, becomes doubly hard to find, except by going distances, when they camp long in one place. But though treated thus unfairly as regards the division of labour, the women can by no means complain of want of devotion to them on the part of the men. Marriages are matters of great solemnity with them, and the tie is strictly kept. Hus-band and wife show great affection for one another, and both agree in extravagant love of their offspring, which they pet and spoil to their heart's content. (68–69)

The initial "buts" in each paragraph create a contrast between Dixie's state-ments and statements made previously by other writers on the region.[6] They also make a comment on "life in general." And the underlying comparison between Victorian life at home and "primitive" life is striking. My paraphrase of the text, if I assume that this contrast is paramount, would be: women work twice as hard because not only do they work in production for the community (or for the system) but also in "household work"; Indian women at least have the compensation of good marriages ("the tie is strictly kept" as opposed to British philandering) and of being able to "pet and spoil their children" (as opposed to the long hours of labor in Britain for working-class children and the "seen-but-not-heard" upbringing of bourgeois and aristocratic children). The elements that appear in my reading of this passage were all prevalent elements of debate in London at the time, especially among feminist and re-formist groups.[7] Paid women's labor in London and in the industrial towns in the north was especially concentrated in activities akin to those performed by the Tehuelche women (weaving and sewing). Male infidelity in all social classes was the silenced issue behind heated debates on prostitution control and legislation on venereal diseases. Dixie's comment on child rearing is the only part of the description in which she is more ambiguous as to moral value, and thus she uses negative words such as "extravagant" and "spoil," even if counterbalanced by positive nouns such as "love" and "heart." The effect of this "extravagant" upbringing is not illustrated by spoiled children, though. On the contrary, Dixie observes that Tehuelche children are amazingly well behaved, and she devotes her most pastoral passage—which I will discuss below—to three Tehuelche children.

What comes immediately after the passage quoted above illustrates the ten-sions within a discourse that while attempting to escape hegemonic constraints returns to them again and again. From the plural "men" and "women," Dixie returns to "the Tehuelche" and then to the generalized pronoun "he," placing the pronoun in a location whose referent is definitely not only male. In this context, Dixie echoes widely described prejudices concerning the Indians:

> The most prominent characteristic of the Tehuelche is *his* easy-going good humour, for whereas most aboriginal races incline to silence and saturnine gravity, *he* is all smiles and chatter. The other good qualities of the race are fast disappearing under the influence of "aquadiente" [*sic*], to the use of which *they* are getting more and more addicted, and soon, it is to be feared, they will become nothing more than a pack of impoverished, dirty, thieving ragamuffins. (121)

Dixie's resistance to prevalent discourses is, of course, problematic since it does not focus on any attempt at social reform or on the creation of alternatives but on a very escapist type of resistance: the creation of Utopian spaces. Like William Henry Hudson, another writer on Patagonia, Dixie draws a Utopian Patagonia that is basically a comment on prevalent problems in Britain, such as the criminal effects of alcohol described in the above passage and a space for self-discovery and self-reflection. The problems with this utilization of the "other" are innumerable: using the space of the "other" for self-reflection or for metaphorical purposes seems to be the underlying link between all colonialist discourses. But while other contemporary texts on Patagonia such as Hudson's *Idle Days in Patagonia* (1893) see "progress" as inevitable, Dixie erases it completely from her descriptions and devotes her descriptive abilities to stressing the "normality" of Indian life—and natural life—when undisturbed by European intervention. This type of descriptive skill is at its best in her pastoral portrayal of a threesome of youngsters in a tent:

> At one of the tents we saw two remarkably clean and pretty girls, who were engaged on some kind of sewing work; and beside them—probably making love to one (or both)—stood an equally good-looking youth, who struck me by the peculiar neatness of his dress, and his general "tiré à quatre épingles" appearance. His hair was brushed and combed, and carefully parted,—*a bright red silk handkerchief* keeping its glossy locks in due subjection. His handsome *guanaco capa* was new, and brilliantly painted on the outside, and being half opened, displayed a clean white chiripá, fastened at the waist by a silver belt *of curious workmanship.* A pair of neatly fitting horsehide boots encased his feet, reaching up to the knees, where they were secured by a pair of *gay-coloured garters,* possibly the gift of one of the *fair maidens* at his side. (71–72)

What is going on in this description? Why is Dixie so intent on drawing a picture of spiritual bliss which, except for the few Indian elements that appear almost as superimpositions on the text, seems to be extracted from a Thomas Hardy novel? Again, what strikes me most in this description is Dixie's ability to see the "other" as familiar. But in choosing a pastoral tone, she is situating her characters in an irrecoverable past tense. Like Hardy, she is fatalistically narrating a present becoming past. Hardy's complaint that "if the true artist ever weeps it probably is then, when he discovers the price he has to pay for the privilege of writing in the English language" holds true for Dixie. The constraints of the imperial language and of the literary tropes of writing on the "other" are, for her, insurmountable. But unlike Hardy, Dixie is not aware of these constraints. Her book finishes on a light note:

> Taking it all in all, it was a very happy time, and a time on whose like I would gladly look again. (251)

This light ending is highly problematic considering the extent of the massacre which was going on at the time. Dixie's visit to Patagonia happened during General Julio Argentino Roca's Campaign to the Desert, and it was openly discussed and celebrated in the Argentine press and in the European geographical journals where many travel writers first published their works. Through her omission of all references to military campaigns, Dixie creates an elaborate discursive space for the Indians to live in but does not assign them any actual real geographical or historical place in which to continue living. Her romanticized depictions of Indian life do nothing else than grant her a space from which to narrate her own self.

5

Traveling/Teaching/Writing: Jennie Howard's
In Distant Climes and Other Years

By the late nineteenth century, unchaperoned women travelers to Argentina had been warned of the possibility of being abducted and forced into prostitution. Massive campaigns were orchestrated outside Argentina to put an end to white slavery. Unsuccessful as these campaigns were, they brought to the attention of European and U.S. citizens the imminent danger that the country posed for unsuspecting young women. Donna Guy has analyzed how campaigns against white slavery were tainted by racism on the part of Europeans who shuddered at the thought of European white women having sex with men of other races. Legalized prostitution in Argentina and campaigns against it both inside and outside Argentina brought to light contradictions intrinsic in both the constructions of nationalism in Argentina and in the constructions of the different European nationalisms in the contact zones: Argentine nationalism as always threatened by foreign interference; European nationalisms in danger of being contaminated by nonwhite ethnicities.[1]

One of Guy's most emphatic claims in her analysis of prostitution is that foreign prostitutes were very few in comparison to Argentine-born ones and that the anxiety about importation of prostitutes was related to other issues such as the xenophobia that resulted from massive immigration. The debate about female prostitution spilled over into a more general debate on female labor and on foreign female laborers. The authorities on female issues were the members of the Society of Beneficence, a charity institution organized by Bernardino Rivadavia in 1823 and which since national reunification had become increasingly powerful and influential. In a country which was modernizing itself at notable speed, these women represented the amalgam of values associated with the colonial Hispanic past. They objected to female labor and mistrusted foreigners. Their strongholds—the education of girls and women and the health care of women and children—allowed them to exercise an inordinate amount of power over the lives of both native and foreign-born Argentineans. Interestingly enough, their position of power was only marginally affected by the prostitutes, but it was dramatically changed by other unchaperoned women travelers—North American normal school teachers.

The connection between teaching and prostitution as professions reserved for women is made by Redding S. Sugg in his preface to *Motherteacher: The Feminization of American Education:*

> The first profession opened to women consisted of the sale of sexual love and was called prostitution; the second, an initiative of nineteenth-century Americans, was a traffic of maternal love and was called pedagogy. (7)

This quotation opens up noteworthy issues in the discussion of the importation of teachers that Domingo Faustino Sarmiento set up to educate the country and the definition of the profiles of teachers, in particular, and female workers in general. Sugg shows how the formation of normal schools in the United States required a definite change in direction in what education meant and how it was carried out on a day-to-day basis: when most teachers were male, physical punishment was an integral part of education; however, when normalism introduced female teachers into the education of teenage boys, there was a shift to a pedagogy which shunned physical punishment and stressed the affective, in what Sugg calls "a traffic of maternal love." This model, which was transplanted to Argentina by Sarmiento, shaped the educational system like a family: the paterfamilias-administrator was a man, the teacher in charge of the daily contact with the children was a woman, and the patriarch-fathers who presided over the whole arrangement were the "fathers of education": Horace Mann in the United States, Sarmiento in Argentina. Sarmiento describes with loaded metaphors his plan to educate the country using North American teachers:

> Está pues el terreno preparado para sembrar la semilla, la buena semilla que traen las maestras. Desde allí él extenderá sus ramas por toda la República y San Juan será por segunda vez, el Precursor de la nueva doctrina. En mi viaje he sentido, palpado, que la educación será en el ánimo del pueblo y que la tierra, el espíritu, serán igualmente cultivados.
>
> Sarmiento (letter to Mary Mann dated February 15, 1870)

[The land is therefore ready to sow the seed, the good seed that the teachers bring. From there, branches will spread all over the Republic and San Juan will be for the second time, the Precursor of the new doctrine. In my trip, I have felt that education will belong in the spirit of the people and that the land and the spirit will be equally cultivated.]

This quotation presents a development of Sarmiento's perception of the land in *Facundo* where he establishes a relationship between the landscape and the people and notes how the absence of a traveler/social analyst interferes with the possibility of prescribing a "correct drug" for the problem of the nation, a "drug" which would address the misgivings and limitations of the country in the context of what the nation needs according to its geography. In his letter to Mary Mann, Sarmiento acknowledges the advantages granted to him by the end of his exile. He now can travel the land, question it, examine its signs, and uncover the "right drug" to cure the ills of the nation: education. Absolutely reliant on his sight, Sarmiento reads the signs and reports on a land ready for planting. The farmers—U.S. teachers—are very much like the farmers he wanted for the actual—and not the metaphorical—land: white and Anglo-Saxon.[2] What is unusual in this farming metaphor is that the planting is done by women—"las maestras." Sarmiento did hire men as well as women, but he makes his point dramatically clear when he chooses the feminine noun here: his educational project was to be carried out by women partially masculinized by their professional undertakings and devoid of the Catholicism prevalent among the Argentinean upper-class women from the Society of Beneficence, who still had a firm grip on education. The fact that Sarmiento envisioned this project as resulting in a fruitful harvest of millions of female teachers must have seemed radical to the Society ladies who saw their otherwise undisputed control over the minds of young women slip through their fingers.

In purging Argentinean education of its religiosity, Sarmiento expected to attract the Anglo-Saxon immigrants he envisioned as instrumental in the construction of a modern Argentina. The trip Sarmiento refers to in the third quotation took him to Córdoba, Santa Fe, and Entre Ríos, and Sarmiento devoted a large part of the letter to Mary Mann describing the German and Swiss colonies where Sarmiento claimed people were happy and rich. This mini-manifesto for universal and lay education is expressed in evangelical terms: "el terreno preparado para sembrar la semilla" [the land is ready for sowing], "la buena semilla" [the good seed], "el Precursor de la nueva doctrina" [the Precursor of the new doctrine]. The whole spirit of the paragraph evokes religious images, and Sarmiento sets himself in the place of a modern prophet: a prophet of secularism.

The Teachers

Jennie Howard was one of these farmers. Jennie Howard never went back "home" to the United States and like many of her colleagues and most of the foreign prostitutes made her home in Argentina. Of the three women I talk about in this part of my study, Howard is the only one who prioritizes her profession, who travels for professional reasons, and who is totally plebeian in the way she addresses her job and her writing. Her position in both her own society and in Argentinean society depends absolutely on her own capabilities as a teacher—something she has trained for and which has become her whole life. Her own account is not personal in intent but meant to account for a whole group of men and principally women who, like her, carried out Sarmiento's educational project. All in all, sixty-five North American teachers founded or reorganized eighteen normal schools in Argentina between the years 1869 and 1898. About a third of them stayed in the country for good and continued teaching either in public or in private schools.

In 1842, while exiled in Chile, Sarmiento had founded a normal school only two years after Horace Mann's foundation of the first normal school in the United States. In *La educación popular* published in 1849, he advocated universal lay education. During the early 1850s, in an extended trip to the United States, Sarmiento visited schools, gathered books and materials, and interviewed educators and teachers. Having already decided that Argentina's schools would emulate their American counterparts, Sarmiento still had to choose a specific model and get the human-power to put it into practice. For the model he chose Chicago; for teachers, he chose women. Women were preferred because, as Mann had pointed out to him, they could be hired for a fraction of a man's salary. Sarmiento did not stop there; he described desirable teachers in these terms:

> The girls must be normal-trained, with considerable teaching experience. They must have irreproachable morals and manners. They must come from good families. They must be young and good-looking if possible. (Luiggi, *Sixty-Five Valiants* 17–18)

It is clear how much Sarmiento's project shared elements of the educational project of the elite women, even when it definitely came up against it. The emphasis on the appearance and morals of the "'girls'" was shared by the elites, but the difference was that whereas for the elite women this composure came from Catholicism, for Sarmiento it was an integral part of the education of teachers rooted in a Puritan work ethic and in the Puritan New England ideology of passionlessness to which I will refer later on.

After several false starts and numerous complications attended to by Sarmiento himself, the teachers finally started arriving and occupying posts at normal schools all over the country. Some men were brought to head schools for boys, but the bulk of the teachers were young women from the East Coast and the Midwest of the United States. Jennie Howard was a Bostonian, one of the two Bostonians who according to Alice Luigi had annoyed their Midwestern compatriots with their belief in the academic superiority of their city of origin. Educated at Framingham Normal School, Jennie Howard led a life until her arrival in Argentina that was not very different from that of many of the other teachers. Orphaned after her father had lost his fortune, she needed to look for a means to pay for her brother's Ivy League education as well as to support herself and her older sister.

By the time Howard arrived in Buenos Aires, she was already thirty-eight and an experienced teacher. Together with another Bostonian—Edith Howe —she organized the Girls' Normal School of Corrientes. From there she went on to the Girls' School of Córdoba and to the coeducational ("mixta") school of San Nicolás. When she retired, she was a methodology teacher, and the minister of education, Juan Ramón Fernández, granted her a special retirement.

Howard's "Distant Climes"

The title Howard chose for her book *In Distant Climes and Other Years* has definite connections with the title of a book by a compatriot of hers and Argentina's ultimate expatriate writer: William Henry Hudson's *Far Away and Long Ago*. The deictic position from which Hudson and Howard write is however very different: Hudson writes in England as an adult about the place where he spent his childhood; Howard distances herself from Argentina ("in distant climes"), which is the place from where she is writing this book (a memoir? A travelogue?). By the time she writes it, Howard has spent more than half of her life in Argentina and yet she chooses a foreigner's perspective for her writing. The place where she has chosen to spend her life is still foreign. In spite of remarkable progress, it is still a land populated by unreliable inhabitants who speak a "jibberish [*sic*]" language.

Howard's book starts off using one of the conventions of travel writing by historicizing her arrival in Argentina in the context of what her U.S. compatriots knew about the country at that time:

> In the United States forty-six years ago, a geographical knowledge of the
> Argentine Republic even among teachers, was confined mostly to the ancient name of Patagonia, seen on the maps of South America in the geog-

raphies of that time with the strange name of Buenos Aires, pronounced by them "Bonus Airs" stretching across the center of it, and to pictures in the same books of long lines of bullock carts crossing interminable plains. But so far away seemed these distant, mythical lands, and so little information was aroused as to where these bullock carts were going or from whence they came. (23)

This mythical and romanticized description of the country has nothing in common with what will be Howard's own descriptions. Howard does not romanticize the region and rarely finds any beauty in it. On the contrary, her description points to the end of the order of the open pampas traveled by bullock carts. What she sees in the country is backwardness and barbarism, and her greatest achievement is her own participation in putting an end to this barbarism through the civilizing efforts of education. Unlike Dixie and Beck-Bernard, Howard does not devote any time to describing Indians or gauchos. Completely identified with Sarmiento's project, Howard sees education as the tool which will push Argentina into modernity and which will rescue it from its position among the "mythical" and "distant" (that is, uncivilized, barbaric) places. In this process of modernization, the indigenous populations had no place, and Howard does not even devote a deprecatory remark to them. She does, however, engage in long descriptions of insects who stand in the way of civilization, going even as far as eating volumes of Dickens's novels.

It is not surprising in the context of Howard's identification with capitalism and modernization that she will use Charles Dickens as her literary mentor. On the way to Buenos Aires, she writes, the teachers stopped in "delightful London with its historical associations known to them only through books," (25) where they visited "some of the haunts of Dickens" (25). Howard reads, celebrates, and shares in Dickens's admiration—but none of his scorn—for modernity, and in her writing she imitates his style. Nowhere is this clearer than in chapter 14, where she triumphantly describes the change Argentina had gone through in the previous thirty years. Howard uses fast-paced prose to praise the new Argentina (especially the new Buenos Aires), full of department stores, connected by fast and modern means of transportation, and generally buzzing with activity. She celebrates the fact that this change has also brought about a change in manners, especially in the way women can lead their lives. In spite of this change which she terms a "Rip van Winkle" awakening, she does not compare Buenos Aires to London but to "gay Paris." There is an intrinsic contradiction in Howard's discourse: by refusing to equate Buenos Aires to London, she is steadfastly holding on to the belief that the London she has read in Dickens coexists with the London of culture, with precapitalist London. Buenos Aires falls short because the new order has no previous glorious order to coexist with:

> The men in general dedicate themselves wholly to business and to the pleasures of life, and are materialists, neglecting the higher questions of soul and spirit; and lofty ideas have little attraction for them. Argentina has given birth to a poet now and then or a writer of spiritual thought, but they do not seem to have succeeded in impressing their standards upon the masses. In many literary and artistic societies, the spirit of materialism reigns as it also does in great educational institutions. (119)

Passionlessness and the Teacher

Howard's greatest feat might well be that she is able to write a whole book about herself from her point of view using the pronoun "I" only once.[3] Whereas Beck-Bernard's prose effaces the existence of a husband and, at a lesser level, of children, Howard's prose effaces the very voice that engendered it. Howard's experience is therefore normalized and generalized. To avoid using the first person, she cumbersomely uses all the different passive and impersonal forms available as well as of the third person plural in nouns such as "the teachers" and "the American teachers." In the chapter "American Teachers Make Dreams, Realities," she narrates her own experience on the way to Paraná (her first appointment):

> Once fairly settled, they set about absorbing as much of the Spanish language as possible in four months. The days were dedicated to hard study, visiting the Normal School frequently to accustom the ear to the sound of Spanish, and having two teachers, one for grammar and one for conversation. (40)

Her style becomes cumbersome at times because of her insistence on keeping it impersonal and general (talking of herself, for example, she says "one of the American teachers had the great honor and pleasure of being received in the home of the General Mitre . . ." [97]). In effacing others, she effaces herself. No one has a name in her narrative except the great male "heroes"—Sarmiento, Mann, Mitre. The teachers recover their names only in the last chapter where they are listed and grouped into different categories.

It might be argued that this self-effacement is part of the normal school education. Teachers—both the North American teachers and their Argentine disciples—were supposed to elaborate a complex duality between their public and their private lives. Jennie Howard's narrative transfers the pedagogic ethos to her own writing, and presumably to her own life too. Even the physical discomfort she feels has to be erased. Howard's presentation of herself is completely devoid of sentiment. She is the professional woman, the traveler with a mission. The impersonality of the teacher as professional is what is going to protect her from the dangers of contamination by the outside world.[4]

Underlying Howard's discourse is the ideology of passionlessness. Nancy F. Cott has shown how this ideology, which was prevalent in New England from the end of the eighteenth century until the mid-nineteenth century, was widespread among middle-class women, allowing them to have professional endeavors beyond the family and to define the size and structure of the family. According to Cott:

> The ideology of passionlessness, conceived as self-preservation and social advancement for women, created its own contradictions: on the one hand, by exaggerating sexual propriety so far as to immobilize women and, on the other, by allowing claims of women's moral influence to obfuscate the need for other sources of power. The assertion of moral integrity within passionlessness had allowed women to retrieve their identity from sexual vulnerability and dependence. (236)

Cott's article stresses the instrumental role that Protestantism played in the formation of this ideology by portraying women as more spiritual than men on the condition that they renounce their sexuality. This new perspective on women made possible the reformation of education carried out in the middle of the eighteenth century in the United States and the importation of U.S. teachers into Argentina later on. In Argentina, these women whom Sarmiento described as possessing "irreproachable morals" found opposition especially among the traditional Catholic groups for whom all sources of morality had to come from the Catholic church. The teachers had, in turn, to educate their female students in this ideology of passionlessness as an essential element to the successful outcome of an education that would possibly uproot them from their parents' home and grant them financial independence.

The Family

The text establishes a family relationship between Sarmiento, the teachers, and the students. Sarmiento was "the father of Argentine education," an image which by the 1930s when this book was published was fairly widespread. But let us look at other ways in which Howard describes him:

> Perhaps those who may read these chronicles, while passing by this statue thinking of the splendid heroic figure for which it stands, may give a thought to the band of self-sacrificing American women who answered his

call and followed his lead into his own far land, and ably seconded and made practical his enthusiasm. (42)

If the word "women" was replaced by "woman," it would unequivocally stand for "his wife." The statue Howard is referring to is Sarmiento's in Boston (her hometown). The reference to the teachers as multiple wives who follow Sarmiento and put his plans into practice is noteworthy; after all, Howard herself claims that the first teacher who went to Argentina and returned to the United States to recruit more teachers had an encouraging "robust glow." This familial structure and its underlying ideology of passionlessness will survive well into the twentieth century, transmitted from generation to generation of men and especially women in normal schools.

Jennie Howard's written account of her experiences was not published until 1931, but in her experiences she is a precursor to the women writers I discuss in Part 3. Howard is a professional, a single woman traveling by herself with a personal plan that went beyond marriage and children. Her role as a government-appointed employee put her in a privileged position in the country in which she arrives without previous knowledge of its idiosyncrasies or language.[5] The type of female subjectivity which she deploys in her writing was one of the cornerstones of women's education at the beginning of the twentieth century. The liberal elite's commitment to women's education would eventually warrant the inclusion of millions of immigrant women into lettered culture.

3

Shifting Identities, 1900–1930

6

Traveler/Governess/Expatriate: Emma de la Barra's *Stella*

En la escritora gentil hay una "brava" ciudadana.
[In the gentile woman writer there is a "spirited" citizen.]
Edmundo D'Amicis, prologue to *Stella*

In 1905, *Stella,* a novel published by Emma de la Barra under the pseudonym César Duayen, became the first Argentinean best-seller. The main character in the novel is Alejandra Fussell, the daughter of an Argentinean woman of the elite and a Norwegian scientist. After her father's death, Alejandra (or Alex, as she is mostly referred to in the novel) travels to Argentina with her younger invalid sister Stella, whom she has raised since her mother's death. Following her father's wishes, the sisters move in with their dead mother's brother and his family. Intelligent and educated, Alex becomes her cousins' governess and arouses emotions of admiration and jealousy. Courted by several successful men, Alex falls in love with her aunt's brother, Máximo Quirós, a rich heir who spends his life traveling. The lovers finally get together but only after Máximo has undertaken civic responsibilities in the construction of the nation.

Stella engages actively with issues of gender and citizenship. Even though the book is narrated from a third person omniscient point of view, the reader is encouraged to sympathize with Alex and to participate in her profound critique of upper-class life in Buenos Aires. A main focus of the critique is the ignorance which riddles the women of the elite. De la Barra distinguishes between education ("educación") and upbringing ("instrucción"), and unlike all the other women in the novel, Alex has both: her European scientist father's knowledge and her Argentine mother's moral and religious principles. As a cultural "mestiza,"[1] Alex is both an insider and a visitor in Argentinean culture, and as a woman who is both educated and "instruida" she is a catalyst for change. The men who fall in love with her realize that they have to become better men (and better citizens) to deserve her.

De la Barra seems to indicate that to synthesize the European and the autochthonous as Alex does is very difficult. As a matter of fact, traveling in itself does not help achieve this combination since it only results in ". . . esa instrucción superficial de los que han viajado mucho" (96) [. . . that superficial education of those who have traveled a lot]. Alex's mother, Ana María, is portrayed as never having profited from the knowledge that her husband (and Europe) had to offer. Her ignorance is tempered by her piety, and Alex takes from her the latter but discards the former. Alex's identity is a composite of the identities of her father and her mother, her trip to Argentina representing the realization of both her parents' wishes: her father's written wish that the daughters go back to their mother's family; the mother's mandate to return, which she uttered before her death.

Alex also brings her mother's exile full circle: her mother, the text explains, always yearned for a return, but it is going to be the daughters who return to Buenos Aires: Stella to die, Alex to live. Alex's first trip to Argentina is completed with her sister's death. Her second trip, back from Norway (where she has been working as a teacher) to the "estancia," to recover her sister's body for burial in Europe, is left unfinished because she joins Máximo, now a serious citizen. How the love affair develops is left unsaid. The novel ends when Alex goes into the sanatorium for poor children that Máximo built in honor of Stella and which would open only if Alex agrees to run it.

Travel as trope figures prominently in the novel: both Máximo and Alex are experienced travelers who also write. Alex is collecting her father's unpublished work which she will publish as a scientific treatise. Until he meets Alex, Máximo is the dissolute traveler to which references abound in Argentine literature of the time. Alex, on the other hand, travels with her father to study and to learn. Her writing, although it comes from the heart, is not emotional but scientific and didactic; its main function is to honor her father and record *his* voice:

Mi trabajo es material únicamente; interpreto lo que tan sólo El podía concebir. . . . Enhebro sus perlas de Oriente en el miserable hilo de que yo dispongo. (226)

[My job is only material; I interpret what only He could imagine. . . . I thread his pearls of the Orient on the miserable thread that I own.]

Alex's fascination with patriarchal authority permeates the novel and takes other manifestations: Argentina is represented as lacking the moral authority of a father figure, and Máximo is a worthy suitor for Alex only after he has applied his money to help others and his privilege and education to become

> el jefe y guía de la numerosa y selecta agrupación que ayudaba con desinterés y patriotismo a su país, en la evolución que él muchos años antes profetizara. (388)

> [the chief and guide of the numerous and select group that helped their country with disinterest and patriotism, in the evolution that he had prophesied many years earlier.]

The preoccupations with authority, education, and national identity which organize the narrative in *Stella* are indicative of the spirit of the time, and the crisis that Alex observes reflects a larger crisis in the nation, a crisis Máximo explains in these terms:

> Avanzamos por agregación y adopción, lo que nos va quitando todo lo nuestro. La nómina de los concurrentes a cualquier fiesta le dice a usted cómo nos eliminamos. Los nietos de las grandes familias, que no han sabido mantener el rango de sus ascendientes, se substituyen por los inmigrantes, enérgicos y luchadores pero sin alma nacional, con el patriotismo estrecho vinculado a la prosperidad material únicamente. De ahí la indiferencia que permite todos los abusos y las tiranías solapadas, y la relajación moral. (234)

> [We are advancing through addition and adoption, which are taking away all that is our own. The list of guests at any party shows you how we are eliminating ourselves. The grandchildren of the great families that have not known how to maintain the rank of their ancestors are being replaced by immigrants, who fight and are energetic, but do not have a national soul. Their thin patriotism is connected only to material prosperity. From there comes the indifference that allows for all of the abuses and evasive tyrannies, as well as moral relaxation.]

De la Barra makes a rather naive and ambivalent suggestion of what men should do, but she is very assertive in her recommendations for improving their lot. Basically, women should be more like Alex. They should be educated and "instruidas," have access to the liberal professions, and disdain luxury and idleness. They should have freedom within the public sphere and be queens inside the home. Like Alex, women should be a compound of the technological advances of Europe and the spiritual virtues of pre-immigration Argentina.[2]

As a couple, Máximo and Alex represent the possibility of an auspicious future for the country. Alex, who stands for the best of bourgeois northern Europe (science, technology, hard work) and the best of Argentinean femininity (religiosity, charity), marries Máximo, who by the end of the novel has added the characteristics of good citizen to the material qualities he has always had, mainly "old money" and land. In Alex, her mother's European journey closes, since Alex returns to "una casa como en la que nació mamá" [a house like the one in which Mother was born], the endogamous quality of Argentina's landowners as evident as ever in a marriage that binds again the same two families that Alex's aunt and uncle had joined.

In dealing so strongly with the problematics of the time and offering possible solutions, *Stella* emerges out of the spirit of the period; and as a publishing boom it undoubtedly provided a starting point for other texts. In a study of weekly periodical fiction in the period of 1917–27 (a genre that shares many conventions with a realist novel such as *Stella*), Beatriz Sarlo has pointed out:

> la ficción y también la poesía no sólo se construyen con materiales ideológico-experienciales que, de algún modo, forman parte de un patrimonio común transformado estéticamente, sino que los textos mismos funcionan como formadores activos de fantasías sociales. Identificaciones morales y psicológicas se suscitan en el proceso de lectura y es posible pensar que tengan una permanencia más duradera que la del momento del consumo y el placer. Huellas de la literatura en sus lectores y también marcas de los lectores en la literatura. (*Imperio* 23)

> [fiction as well as poetry are not only constructed with ideologic-experiential materials that in some way form part of a common aesthetically transformed patrimony, but also the texts themselves function as active shapers of social fantasies. Moral and psychological identifications are sustained in the reading process and it is possible to think that they have a more lasting presence than that of the moment of consumption and pleasure. Traces of literature in its readers and also marks of the readers in the literature.]

Stella's main contribution to Argentine literature is the inclusion of a strong-willed independent woman as a protagonist. Alex's responsibility as the inscriber of her father's words and as the record keeper of her adoptive family's finances inaugurates an era when women of all social classes will be present in the public sphere. De la Barra's novel also engages with the heated debates on the feasibility of modernization in the country. De la Barra's text includes a model of modernization which would not only import European models but also adapt them to the local context. Máximo and Alex stand for the new modern man and woman who could carry out this plan: a moral landowning politician and an educated and modern angel of the house, able to live on her own but virtuous enough to use all her science and knowledge in the home.

7

Globe-Trotting Single Women

For the Spanish American writer, globe-trotting,
at the turn of the century, is the mark of modernity.

Sylvia Molloy, *At Face Value: Autobiographical Writing in Latin America*

The year is 1910. Argentina sets out to celebrate the hundredth anniversary of the May Revolution and a hundred years of independent life. This celebration, which will be known in Argentina as the centennial, served the country as an occasion to evaluate the past, the present, and the future. It was also an excuse to tally the republic's achievements vis-à-vis its European counterparts. A long list of events was organized to celebrate the anniversary and to praise the young republic and its achievements. The general spirit of the centennial was internationalist, its main objective to show how Argentina could interact in a status of equality with the European nations and with the United States.[1]

The centennial was not only a showcase of the achievements of the oligarchic republic but also an occasion in which problems surfaced. Because of the positivistic ideology of the generation of 1880, Argentina had progressed and expanded: it had extended the railways, established a favorable balance of trade, and set up a modern educational system. Argentina had also circumscribed its territories with massive campaigns to displace the indigenous populations and was proceeding to change the characteristics of its population by welcoming hundreds of thousands of European immigrants.[2] The cracks within the system (which was sustained by fraudulently elected governments until 1916) were emerging in the form of labor unrest, strikes, and political instability. A group of intellectuals interpreted the unrest as a crisis of identity and speculated on ways to overcome it. Grouped around the journal *Ideas,* these intellectuals sought to replace the positivistic, lay, and cosmopolitan ideology hegemonic at the time with a new one which would steer Argentina back to the wealth of the Hispanic past. Two of the most active members of the group, Manuel Gálvez and Ricardo Rojas, meditated on the ways in which a nationalist education could make Argentineans out of immigrant children and how a typically Argentinean culture could serve as a unifying language for communication within a nation.

Rojas (1882–1957) designed a program to carry out what he called "la restauración nacionalista" [the nationalist restoration]. For him, the spiritual problem of the nation brought on by modernization and immigration could be solved in the context of liberal democratic values which the public education system had to impose. According to him, public schools were to be the initiators of the "restoration," which would produce a new historical synthesis in which immigrants and their children would be included. The role of the intellectuals was to create a national history and a national literature that would provide the materials by which immigrants would be interpellated into the national identity. Immigrants in this master plan had to give up their idiosyncrasies and their culture to integrate themselves into the nation. An Argentinean history and literature had to be "founded" to provide the canonical contents of the school curriculum.[3] During the 1910s, Rojas held the first chair in Argentine literature at the University of Buenos Aires and wrote the nine-volume *Historia de la literatura argentina.* In his *Restauración nacionalista* (1909), he also hinted at the creation of a national history, and he designed syllabi for the teaching of "modern humanities" (history, geography, literature, "castellano,"[4] "moral cívica") in the different levels of education. For Rojas, who still upheld Sarmiento's categories of civilization and barbarism, sustained change had to be spiritual and independent from modes of production. The restoration could take place in conjunction with the economic system imposed by the liberal government:

> Pero esta restauración del propio pasado histórico debe hacerse para definir nuestra personalidad y vislumbrar su destino. Restaurar el "espíritu tradicional," no significa, desde luego, restaurar sus "formas" económicas o políticas o sociales, abolidas por el proceso implacable y lógico de la civilización. (235)

> [But this restoration of one's own historic past should be done to define our personality and glimpse its destiny. The restoration of the "traditional spirit" does not mean, however, the restoration of its political or social economic "forms" abolished by the relentless and logical process of civilization.]

Rojas, who did not oppose immigration, believed public education was the most important actor in unifying the nation and in creating a new synthesis in a culturally creolized cosmopolitan population. Unlike Rojas, Manuel Gálvez (1882–1962) inverted Sarmiento's categories of civilization and barbarism and located barbarism in the cities and civilization in the provinces which were the stronghold of the Hispanic past. Gálvez develops this idea in his *El diario de Gabriel Quiroga* (1910), which uses the centennial as its background. In *El diario,* a young writer modeled by Gálvez after himself reflects on the crisis which immigration had brought to the country. Buenos Aires and the wealthy provinces of the littoral—which, according to Quiroga/Gálvez, are ugly, libertine, and lacking a physiognomy of their own—are corrupting the country. The provinces of the interior represent everything which is positive: spirituality, religion, the mistrust of foreigners:

> Pero las provincias interiores, libres aún del desborde inmigratorio, ignoran las llagas que nutre con sus vicios la cosmopolita Buenos Aires, y precisamente de las provincias proceden los contados espíritus democráticos que mitigan, con sus prestigios, el descrédito moral de la hora presente. (109)[5]

> [But the interior provinces, still free from the onslaught of immigration, are ignorant to the wounds that cosmopolitan Buenos Aires nourishes with its vices, and precisely out of these provinces emerge the few democratic spirits that, through their good name, mitigate the moral disrepute of the present time.]

The forty years of barbarism are reinterpreted by Quiroga/Gálvez as the rebellion "del espíritu americano contra el espíritu europeo"[6] [of the American spirit against the European spirit]. In the midst of the celebrations (the book finishes on May 25, 1910), Quiroga takes a step back to call attention to the despicable state of affairs and to offer a possibility of revindication in Hispanism, Catholicism, and spiritualism.

In both Rojas's and Gálvez's work, women function as important metaphors for the moral crisis of the nation and its possible solutions. Rojas believed that a new American cultural identity which would be the synthesis of European and indigenous traditions had to be created. The process by which this new culture came to be was depicted by Rojas in heavily gendered metaphors. Women were instruments for the nation, the space where American men could inscribe their own history.[7]

Gálvez devoted several of his works to exploring issues concerning women. His thesis *La trata de blancas* (1905) dealt with prostitution, a subject he would later fictionalize in *Nacha Regules* (1918).[8] He treated normalism and the role of women in education in *La maestra normal* (1914). The protagonist of *La maestra normal,* which takes place in La Rioja, is Raselda, an unsophisticated local teacher who is seduced by a male colleague from the littoral. Raselda becomes pregnant, has an illegal abortion, is removed from her job in the capital city, and is relegated to a rural school. Who is to blame for Raselda's misery? Far from leaving the answer to this question in the hands of the reader, Gálvez makes Raselda herself spell it out:

Aquella tarde que se confesara había comprendido que la religión era la única defensa contra el pecado. Ahora pensaba que si ella hubiera sido verdadera creyentese habría salvado. Pero en la escuela nunca le hablaron de Dios, y algunos profesores hasta le enseñaron a despreciar la religión. (227)

[The afternoon that she confessed she understood religion to be the only defense against sin. Now she thought that if she had been a true believer she would have been saved. But in school they had never spoken of God, and some teachers had even taught her to scorn religion.]

La maestra normal dramatizes several controversial issues of the period such as lay education, the education of women, and the moral decay of the country. It is indicative of Gálvez's ideology that he chose women such as Nacha Regules and Raselda to depict the problems of Argentina. For Gálvez, the instability in the roles of women was an example (and maybe a cause) of the instability of the country. The prostitute and the "fallen" normal school teacher represented for him the emergent elements in a society which had disdained ideals and values. Gálvez's concern with spatial control of women was shared by the women writers I treat in this chapter. Gálvez worried that certain social spaces could contribute to the degeneration of women. Emma de la Barra, Cecilia Grierson, and Ada María Elflein, on the other hand, believe in the defining role of women as creators of adequate spaces for the development of independent women. It is not surprising that the battlefield between both ideologies is fought on the bodies of women and in four distinct spaces: the bourgeois home, the brothel, the normal school, and the controlled yet still not modernized landscape of the western provinces of Cuyo.

The debates on values, nationalism, and education in which Rojas and Gálvez participated inform my discussion of travel literature and women travelers in this part of the book. Since what constituted the national had to be defined vis-à-vis the "other" (which took on different meanings according to who was speaking), travel writing as the genre of the encounter with the "other" continued to be a popular venue for the writings of elite men. The period 1900–1930 also saw a flourishing, which peaked at the time of the centennial, of travel writing on Argentina by foreigners. After the Russian Revolution, left-wing Argentinean writers added their travelogues on the Soviet Union to the corpus.

During this same period, writing by women flourished. Partly a consequence of the general economic prosperity which also accounted for a proliferation of cultural manifestations by men, literature by women also owed its authors and its readers to the educational reforms of the late nineteenth century, especially normalism. The normal school system instituted by Sarmiento was responsible for the education and professionalization of hundreds of lower-middle-class women. By 1910, about 70 percent of the teachers were women. Many of the writers of the period, including Alfonsina Storni, were normal school teachers.[9] Most of the women who participated in the feminist movements at the beginning of the century had also graduated from the normal schools.[10]

The entrance of women into the workforce in large numbers and the modernization of the country also allowed for a larger mobility of women. Chaperoning as a practice was dying out except in the very wealthy traditional families.[11] Middle-class women of immigrant origin enjoyed an unprecedented freedom of movement as well as new educational and professional perspectives. Gina Lombroso Ferrero, an Italian who traveled to Argentina in 1907, wrote in her travelogue:

> I have known in Buenos Aires some forty female doctors who practice medicine, surgery, dentistry, anthropology and obstetrics. I visited a class at the Academy of Medicine which was directed by a woman. I also visited a school of massage and of nursing founded and directed by a woman; and on more than one occasion listened to speeches given publicly by acclaimed and renowned women. (37)

In this context, women also started to travel more and to write about travel. Cecilia Grierson and Julieta Lanteri, both normal school teachers and medical doctors, traveled to Europe to research issues of women's education and women's health, respectively. The first text I analyze in this chapter, Grierson's *Educación técnica de la mujer,* is a result of her European experience. Like Jennie Howard, Grierson traveled on a contract and wrote her book on request, inaugurating professional travel writing for women in Argentina. Ada María Elflein, a teacher and professional writer and journalist, also wrote travel literature by request. Her trip to the west of Argentina was sponsored by the Buenos Aires newspaper *La Prensa,* where her text was published. These authors strive to give satisfactory answers to questions already posed by Emma de la Barra in *Stella:* how can Argentina as a nation construct a discourse that includes and excludes groups of people who are or are not welcome in the nation? what kind of education can be used to make this discourse prevalent in the population? what role do women have within this discourse and within the educational plan that will serve to propagate it?

To Europe and Back: Cecilia Grierson's Professional Trip

John and William Parish Robertson, who visited the River Plate in the 1820s and wrote one of the most often quoted travel books on the region, obtained from Bernardino Rivadavia a piece of land to start the first Scottish colony in Argentina. One of the first families in the colony was that of Cecilia Grierson's grandparents, William and Katherine Grierson. Cecilia Grierson's father, named John Parish Robertson after the traveler, was born in the colony in 1827. Educated in Buenos Aires and Britain, John Parish Robertson Grierson married the daughter of Irish immigrants and settled down on an estancia in Entre Ríos, where their daughter Cecilia was born.

Cecilia Grierson's trajectory is paradigmatic of what the normal school system could do for women. After her father's death, Cecilia worked as a governess, then as a rural teacher in Entre Ríos. She was admitted to the normal school of Buenos Aires at the age of fifteen, graduated at seventeen, and supported herself and her family with her teacher's salary while she attended medical school. The first Argentinean female medical doctor and an active feminist, Grierson founded schools for the blind and for the deaf and several professional schools for women. She also taught at the University of Buenos Aires, organized the Argentine Association of University Women, participated in the International Federation of University Women, and presided over the International Women's Conference which met in Buenos Aires in 1910.

In 1899, Grierson was planning a trip to Europe as a representative of various women's organizations in Argentina, Chile, and Brazil, when the Argentine minister of education commissioned her to do research on the technical and professional education of women. Her book *Educación técnica de la mujer* (1902) was the report on this trip, which she prepared for the Argentinean ministry of education. She was the second woman who was commissioned by an Argentinean government to embark on such a mission and the first one to write a book reporting on a trip.[12] Her trip took her to professional schools for women in Germany, Belgium, Holland, Switzerland, Austria-Hungary, France, England, and Sweden. The names of the countries function as the titles for the different chapters of her book. The introduction lists Grierson's occupations during the two years between the time she traveled to Europe and the time she made the report available. The body of the text consists of a chapter devoted to each country she visited; a two-page chapter titled "Otros países," in which she refers briefly to Denmark, Poland, Russia, and Italy; and a chapter devoted to the United States, which Grierson did not visit. The last chapter of the book, "República Argentina," is the longest. In it Grierson describes a feasible plan for the technical education of women in Argentina. An appendix includes syllabi from different schools.

The similarity between this report and Domingo Faustino Sarmiento's *Educación popular* is overwhelming. *Educación popular,* first published in Santiago in 1849, was a report Sarmiento put together for the Chilean government. The book had been reprinted in Argentina in 1895 as part of Sarmiento's complete works. Like Sarmiento, Grierson includes programs from schools she visited abroad as models for what Argentine education could become. Unlike Sarmiento, who also used experiences from these trips to write his travelogue, Grierson restricts her writings on her experiences abroad to this technical book which was used as a textbook for the training of teachers. Grierson also published several other textbooks for the training of nurses and massage therapists, reports on different aspects of education and health care, and histories of nursing, of the Scottish colony where her father was born, and of the municipality of Buenos Aires. In this study, I will refer both to her *Educación técnica* and to an autobiographical speech she wrote on the occasion of retiring from teaching in 1916.[13] As I will show, this speech illuminates the way in which the personal and the public interact in Grierson's *Educación técnica.*

Cecilia Grierson is the first professional Argentinean female travel writer. As such, her writing shares many characteristics with Jennie Howard's. Although Howard's experience preceded Grierson's by a couple of decades, Grierson's book appeared first. However, the subject position from which Grierson speaks is that of a professional woman, a mode of subjectivity which was inaugurated in the country by North American normal school teachers such as Howard. As a matter of fact, Grierson pays tribute to the North American teachers in her text, calling them "inteligentes, emprendedoras e independientes" (167) [intelligent, enterprising, and independent]. These three adjectives describe the model of femininity that Grierson advocates, and she uses them to describe the end product of her educating mission. They also represent the best attributes a professional traveler like Grierson could have.

In the remainder of this section I will discuss how Grierson writes a travel book in which the very characteristics of the narrative of travel are displaced in favor of a coherent argument to advance a model of education. The trip appears in the background; the particulars of it are never specifically alluded to in a gesture which expresses Grierson's goal: to do away with artifice and the minute details of her daily personal life in favor of the construction of a globalizing project which she sums up in this way:

Desearía ver implantado el amor a la *verdad* y *combatir* nuestra nefasta *tendencia al lujo, la mentira y falsas apariencias.* . . . (207)

[I would like to see love of *truth* implanted [in our students] and I would like to *combat* our harmful *tendency towards luxury, lies and false appearances.* . . .]

The aim is therefore not only to construct an educational model but also to modify an identity which here appears only alluded to as what is "ours." The austerity her book champions is reflected in her very direct and straightforward writing. Her ideal woman, based on the model of femininity of the northern European bourgeoisie, is constructed in opposition to that of upper-class Argentinean women. Her identity as a traveler is written in opposition to that of leisure travelers. Elements from travel writing do appear in her text, and Grierson sets herself up as the model for the professional traveler. Unlike leisure travelers who recommend hotels and restaurants, Grierson gives practical instructions on how to make the most of a research trip:

Por eso, mucho tiempo he perdido y mucho trabajo me ha costado encontrar en cada ciudad las instituciones del hogar y eso conociendo el idioma de cada país, sin lo cual no puede darse un paso adelante. (13)

[Therefore I have lost much time and it has been difficult to find domestic schools in each city and this is all knowing the language of each country without which one could not make any progress.]

It is characteristic of Grierson's writing that she represents herself as able and shows the problem solved rather than the process of solving it. She gives advice (learn a foreign language) in an indirect way, explaining how she set herself up for success. In keeping with the spirit of enterprise, she never discusses how she was actually able to overcome the difficulties. Her reference to languages is equally indirect. Even in her speech, she never accounts for how she learned languages other than her native English ("Fui al examen con una base un poco errática: tres idiomas, siendo el castellano el que menos sabía" [129] [I went to the exam with a somewhat erratic background: three languages, with Spanish being the one I knew least]). Throughout the text, she insists on the need for Argentine teachers to know several languages to be able to travel to Europe to improve their training. Language learning is seen as a means to achieve modernity and is never questioned on nationalistic principles.

It is tempting to speculate on why Grierson did not omit the few references to her trip altogether. The text would have certainly not lost cohesiveness if it had been organized as the result of research and not the result of a research trip. The allusions to the trip, however, position Grierson very differently in relationship to her subject. Being there, as we know, is the key to authority in travel writing, and Grierson uses her short references to travel to claim this interpretive authority: "Como he estado algún tiempo en Amsterdam ..." (69) [As I have spent some time in Amsterdam]; ." ... uno necesita ser presentado o sino escribir a la dirección ..." (123) [one needs to be introduced or if not write down the address]; "Frau Anna Hierta-Retzius a quien conocí en el Congreso de Mujeres en Londres ..." (155) [Frau Anna Hierta-Retzius whom I met at the Women's Conference in London]. These phrases stress Grierson's authority and also implicate her in the project of providing a model for the enterprising, modern Argentine woman. Unlike Jennie Howard who never uses the first person, Grierson uses "I" throughout her text, never once shifting to the impersonal "we." Likewise she never shies away from listing her accomplishments and praising her achievements as a pioneer.

Throughout her text, Grierson chooses European models to copy. Her own identity is modeled on that of the European feminists she admires and in opposition to the upper-class Argentine women she was feuding with at the time for control of the National Council of Women and whom she bitterly attacks in her writing. At the time of the writing of *Educación técnica,* Grierson and other professional women were fighting upper-class women for control of the National Council of Women, which included both feminist organizations and traditional charity organizations such as the Society of Beneficence. At stake were the adherence of Argentina to international suffragist struggles, the commitment to civil rights, and the vote for women at home. The disagreements between the two groups finally brought about a schism, and each group hosted a women's conference in celebration of the centennial in 1910. Grierson was the president of the conference sponsored by the Argentine Association of University Women, an internationalist meeting of mainly professional women who advocated legal reforms for suffrage, better working conditions for women, and more equality in the family. Elflein attended the conference presided over by Grierson, but she also participated in the official women's conference: the "Congreso Patriótico de Señoras de la República Argentina." This conference, organized by upper-class women, most of them active in the Society of Beneficence, was a nationalistic meeting to sing the praises of upper-class patrician women and the ties to the Hispanic past. At the National Congress, women were urged to stay in the house, respect the status quo, and repudiate the campaigns for the vote and civil rights.

The Society of Beneficence counted among its members many writers all the way back to one of its founding members—Mariquita Sánchez. The early twentieth century in Argentina saw a flourishing of personal writing by upper-class women, autobiographical writing which was ultimately meant to be read by others and which dealt with personal matters, leisure, art and literature, social functions, and marriage. Grierson's personal writing is strategically positioned against the writings of these women. Instead of dwelling on immobility and readings, her texts are full of action, the streets, hospitals, and schools: the background for her excursions. There are no references to feelings or bodily sensations; the personal in Grierson's writing is completely sublimated into the professional. It is symptomatic that Grierson's personal narrative is always concerned with movement, new endeavors, new activities. In her speech, she presents herself as a worker, "trabajadora," a term which positions her in opposition to the indolent upper-class women.

For Grierson, inclusion in the Argentine nation is a matter of being civilized. National identity is never questioned in her text because it is assumed as a geographical given, elliptically referred to as "lo nuestro," "nuestro," "nosotros"; Argentina is defined as a country in the process of becoming Europeanized (that is, civilized). Grierson's adherence to a narrative of Europeanness includes a belief in a certain order of nations where the most privileged ones are the "países civilizados" [civilized countries]. Part and parcel of this progress was imperialism and the possession of colonies. Grierson's text reflects the workings of a hegemonic ideology which has bearings on relationships of class, race, and gender. Although Grierson is progressive on issues of gender, she is ultimately biased in terms of relationships of class and race. This is seen very clearly when we compare two quotations from her text:

> Mme. van Treyler y Mlle. Haighton tomaron a su cargo los trabajos industriales de las mujeres de las colonias y especialmente de las indígenas de las Indias Occidentales. (78)

> [Mme. van Treyler and Mlle. Haighton took charge of the industrial work of the women of the colonies and especially the indigenous women of the West Indies.]

> Esta enseñanza ha influido muchísimo en Inglaterra y sus colonias y hay muchísimas mujeres que han hecho su fortuna con el cultivo de flores y huerta, agricultura, la cría del gusano de seda en Australia; la del avestruz en Nueva Zelandia; cabañas en el Canadá. (154)

> [This teaching has had a large influence in England and its colonies and there are very many women who have made their fortune through the cultivation of flowers and orchards, agriculture, the breeding of the silk worms in Australia; that of the ostrich in New Zealand; cabins in Canada.]

The racially based hierarchy between women established in the different quotations above runs throughout her text. In the first quotation, Indian women are presented as needing guidance to do their jobs, as working under tutelage in industrial jobs. Transplanted white women in the second quotation, on the other hand, use their knowledge to become entrepreneurs. The womanhood which Grierson sees as desirable is epitomized by bourgeois European women. Grierson's fierce critique of the Argentine upper class mocks the upper class's belief in their moral superiority and their value as guides for the working class:

> Toca a nuestro "high-life" dar el ejemplo que siempre debe venir de lo alto y tener en cuenta nuestras filantrópicas damas que por la limosna sólo se ayuda a medias; mientras la caridad es completa, enseñando a los pobres a bastarse a sí mismos, dándoles hábitos que los eleven moral e individualmente. (190)

> [We rely on our "high-life" to serve as the paragon that should always come from above, that our philanthropic ladies need to keep in mind when they only partially aid with their hand-outs. Real charity is complete. It teaches the poor to be self-sufficient, giving them habits that elevate them morally and individually.]

The irony in the above piece is, of course, directed at the ladies of the Society of Beneficence. The verb "elevate" illustrates Grierson's uncritical use of the class metaphors prevalent among the high-class women. The critique of the high-class philanthropic society ladies does not include a critique of their class status but rather of how they define this class status. In contrast, Grierson includes numerous examples of European aristocratic women attending technical schools and working. Housework is defined as a natural activity for women of all classes, and the Protestant ethic of the dignity of work pervades Grierson's work. In the context of the presentation of herself as a professional, she uses the word worker—"trabajadora"—which establishes an intimacy between her and working-class women and distances her from Argentinean upper-class women who are always described as indolent. Grierson's self-definition is an out-and-out criticism of the way upper-class women define themselves. Grierson opposes the upper-class women's inactivity to the professional women's movement, and the upper-class women's blood relationships with heroes of independence to the professionals' own personal accomplishments. In this, she is a direct heir of Jennie Howard, an inheritance she prides herself on in both her *Educación* and her autobiographical speech:

> Me hubiera llenado de satisfacción el haber llevado a la meta la primitiva escuela de Buenos Aires ("Escuela de Enfermeras y Masajistas"), donde se

preparaban hombres y mujeres, que creo que se han empleado en todas las reparticiones y hogares de nuestro país y que llamo "mi obra"; pero los obstáculos que encuentra toda "pioner" [*sic*] en su camino han sido insuperables; dos veces que fui a Europa, al volver, encontré la escuela deshecha, y hoy continúa en tal estado. Nuestra manía por la reorganización es fatal para las instituciones; pero la semilla está sembrada y otros recogerán más tarde los frutos, reconociendo que la base en que se fundó la institución es la única verdadera, pues se amolda a nuestras costumbres, a pesar de haber sido copiada de los mejores institutos extranjeros, y sobre la cual espero se afirmen todas las instituciones que surgen, como es actualmente la escuela de la asociación que lleva mi nombre. (133)

[It would have filled me with satisfaction to have reached my goal with the primitive school of Buenos Aires ("School of Nurses and Masseurs"), that prepared both men and women, that I think have been employed in all of the government departments and homes of our country and that I call "my work." But the obstacles that every "pioneer" encounters in his way have been insurmountable. The two times that I went to Europe, I found the school undone upon my return, and today it continues in that state. Our mania for its reorganization is fatal for the institutions, but the seed has been sown and others will later reap its fruit, recognizing that the basis on which the institution was founded as its only true foundation, for it has been adapted to our customs despite having been copied from the best foreign institutes, and I hope that all of the institutions that emerge affirm the quality of the school of the association that bears my name.]

These two paragraphs illuminate the relationships that Grierson establishes between identities. On the one hand, her use of the word "pioneer" to refer to herself is symptomatic of the way she always talks about herself, never ashamed of tooting own horn if she is discussing her work. Furthermore, she uses the word in English, a word that in Argentina at the turn of the century resonated with references to the U.S. westward campaigns. The description of her work is done in the image coined by Sarmiento: the sown seed. In her case, as in Sarmiento's, the seed is foreign, but Grierson claims that it is in accord with what is "ours." The image throws light on Grierson's model of identity. The foreign schools she imitated function as models to which the very elusive Argentinity that Grierson refers to adapts well. Her model for femininity is the northern European bourgeoisie, and in her indefatigable activities as teacher, founder of schools, traveler, and textbook writer, Grierson seeks to produce Argentine women who would replicate the European model.

This lack of preoccupation with the idiosyncratic distinguishes Cecilia

Grierson's work from that of the next writer I treat, Ada María Elflein. In Elflein's work, there is a deep involvement in the debate on nationality and nationalism which became crucial during the centenary. Both Grierson and Elflein participated in the celebrations. Grierson, as was already mentioned, presided over the feminist congress; Elflein attended both but read a paper only at the National Congress. Nothing shows the difference between Ada Elflein and Cecilia Grierson more clearly than the very subject Elflein addressed: the importance of wearing a rosette during patriotic functions. When at the turn of the century Grierson traveled to Europe to find models of womanhood and of women's education to imitate, she could not have anticipated that ten years later her opponents in the National Council of Women, rooted as they were in the past and in the traditional, would actually be at the forefront of political debates. Nothing could be further from her imagination, we might guess, than the fact that professional women of immigrant origin educated in European models, like Ada María Elflein, would participate in the project of defining a national agenda. Elflein's travel writing needs to be read in the context of the new definitions of nation and of national identity that surfaced during the centennial and which became hegemonic during the 1930s. In her work, we witness a shift to the interior, to the provinces, to the creole. For the first time, an Argentinean woman travel writer will speak actively of nationality and will give content to a definition of Argentinity. Yet, within this writing preoccupied with the nation, there is also in embryo a new model of femininity which allows for more sexual and physical freedom for women.

Into the Land/Nation: Ada María Elflein Travels to the Heartland

When Ada María Elflein was born in Buenos Aires in 1880, Cecilia Grierson was already twenty-one, the director of a normal school, and a high school biology teacher who was considering becoming a medical doctor. Far from being anecdotal, their age difference helps account for the different outlook each author had on nationalism. Elflein is the first author treated in this study for whom the definition of Argentinity is important. Born right after the Campaign to the Desert, in a country which had already circumscribed its territories, Elflein came of age at a time when railways were uniting the country for the first time and free lay education for all was becoming a reality. Together with these achievements came the interrogation of what these measures of progress were doing for the country and how the numerous immigrants could be made part of the nation.

The first normal schools established by Sarmiento, like the one where Grierson studied, had almost no typically "Argentinean" elements. The Escuela de Paraná, the model for all the Argentinean normal schools, offered only two courses on Argentinean history out of a total of one hundred and twenty required courses. As late as 1877, 85.4 percent of students attending normal schools in the littoral did not study Argentine history and 77.1 percent did not study geography. This started to change in the 1880s when the introduction of a capitalist mode of production in Argentina and the massive arrival of immigrants required the creation of an imagined community in which both the newcomers and most conservative inhabitants of the provinces would be included. The new Argentine nation, with the state as its political entity and education as its interpellating force, created a narrative of Argentinity which challenged other identities such as regional identities, ethnicity, and national origin. To this end, the 1420 law of free, obligatory, and lay education was passed in 1883. The school programs were changed: in the national schools the number of hours devoted to Argentine and American history was increased: in 1874 there were four weekly hours of Argentine and American history and eight hours of general history; in 1888 seven and a half and six and a half, respectively, and the relationship between hours devoted to Argentine and American history and general history had reversed with twelve hours for the former, six for the latter (Tedesco 97). Furthermore, the study of foreign languages had decreased from 24 percent to 14 percent in the period 1874–88 (Tedesco 70).[14]

Ada María Elflein's literary project was foregrounded by the changes in the educational system and the preoccupation with Argentinean (rather than cosmopolitan, modern, European) education. The daughter of German immigrants and a professional writer of children's stories and of nonfictional "criollista" writings on the Argentine landscape and its inhabitants, Elflein had training as a teacher but gave up teaching early in life when through a recommendation of General Bartolomé Mitre, she got a full-time job as a reporter for *La Prensa*. Most of her writings were first published in *La Prensa* in the form of travel accounts, short stories, or "tradiciones." Elflein was a professional writer who wrote profusely and regularly. Her writing was fully devoted to finding a definition of nationality that would serve her—a daughter of immigrants—and in this sense, her definition of nationality is very different from that of most of the members of the National Council of Women. Unlike them, Elflein has no historical ties to the land. In her writing she struggles to create these ties, to write them, and hence her insistence on stressing the Argentinean element of landscapes and characters. Elflein is also the first Argentinean female traveler who can be included in the list of adventurers.[15] She visited Uruguay, Chile, and the Andes, and she descended into mines, traveled on horseback, ventured into the jungle in Misiones, and climbed the Cerro Pelado. If her originality as a traveler is shown in her explorations, it is also clear in her choice of destinations which in itself bears testimony to an increasing engagement with the definition of the nation.

The work I will analyze here is made up of a series of weekly travel articles that Elflein wrote for *La Prensa* during the months of April and May of 1918. At the time of her death in 1919, she had planned to compile the articles into a book under the title *Por campos serranos*.[16] The series had the objective of

> divulgar los conocimientos sobre diversas regiones de nuestro país interesantes por su belleza, por sus recuerdos históricos, riquezas naturales o por cualquier otro atractivo. (April 8)

> [spreading knowledge about diverse regions of our country that are interesting because of their beauty, their historical memories, their natural riches or for whatever other attractive element.]

Other objectives mentioned include luring tourists into regions which were not easily reachable by railway and encouraging women to travel unchaperoned. In this quotation, which will be further analyzed later on, Elflein's feminism and independence are associated with the modern nation and are posited in opposition to the Hispanic past:

> Aparte de los propósitos ya expresados me guiaba en este viaje—como en los anteriores—el interés de animar a nuestras mujeres a deponer sus temores y lanzarse a viajar, no diré solas, pero de dos, o tres, o cuatro, independientes y movedizas, olvidadas de prejuicios y falsos escrúpulos, valientes, briosas y alegres. ¡Cuántas señoras y niñas pasan el verano tristemente en sus casas por no tener un padre, un hermano o un esposo para acompañarlas! Pienso que si se reuniesen, formaran grupos pequeños o grandes comitivas, prescindieran de las tradiciones moriscas y salieran a gozar de las bellezas de nuestra tierra, pronto adquirirían la convicción de que en todo momento las rodeaba y protegía la exquisita cultura argentina. (April 8)

> [Apart from the already expressed objectives I was guided—as I have been previously—by an interest in encouraging our women to lay down their fears and embark on trips, I will not say alone, but in groups of two or three or four, independent and mobile, forgetful of their prejudices and false scruples, brave, enthusiastic and happy. How many ladies spend their summers sadly at home without a father, a brother, or a husband to accompany them! I think that if they got together, they would form small groups or large processions, they would do away with the Moorish traditions and would go out and enjoy the beauty of our land. Soon they would acquire the conviction of being surrounded and protected at every moment by exquisite Argentinean culture.]

The underlying definition of national identity which appears in the paragraph above is a conflation of the vision of nation espoused by the participants of the two women's congresses Elflein attended in 1910. On the one hand, it echoes the involvement of the National Congress with the interior and the return to the land; on the other it champions a model of womanhood which the members of the internationalist feminist conference applauded. The "other" in Elflein's text is the Moor (morisco), a reference to the Hispanic past but also to the "other" of the Hispanic past. In this way, she can reconcile the two ideologies (in the same way she reconciled them by attending the two conferences) and include modern unchaperoned women of immigrant origin into the nation.

The modern woman, whom Elflein envisions as also the patriotic woman, takes elements from the Hispanic past (a system of values, an attachment to the land) and integrates them with the positive elements of northern European feminism (freedom of movement, intelligence). This modern patriotic woman has enough freedom of movement to travel, but in doing so she does not look for foreign models to imitate but rather for what is "Argentinean." Elflein uses the adjective "Argentinean," even in contexts in which it is completely redundant, to stress the existence of a national (albeit unstable) unifying entity.

Gender Trouble

Ada María Elflein is an interesting figure to consider the intersections of gender and nation in Argentina during the first two decades of the twentieth century. Elflein is traditionally seen as a proto-nationalist even when a detailed analysis of her work shows important areas of disagreement with the nationalists of the time, especially in terms of gender. I want to suggest that Elflein constructed a self-image as the rural teacher surrounded by children in order to create an interstitial space in the society of the time to lead an independent life. Joan Rivière defined femininity as a masquerade that a woman chooses in order to disclose and present herself within the confines of patriarchal society. In her analysis of Gabriela Mistral, Licia Fiol-Mata investigates the ways in which Mistral uses patriarchal discourse to create for herself a space in which she is free from the determinants of patriarchal mores. According to Fiol-Mata, Mistral echoes heterosexist and procreationist ideologies to present herself as the teacher of America and the mother of the continent in public, in order to be able to avoid marriage and motherhood and to be a lesbian in private. In this sense, Fiol-Mata contends, gender serves as a closet to Mistral. Elflein uses similar tactics to those employed by Mistral. Like Mistral, she defines herself as a teacher; she does not teach, however, but rather uses her education as a teacher to become completely involved in literature. In her private life, Elflein presents herself as a single woman who lives for decades with a female best friend. Julieta Gómez Paz, Elflein's biographer, describes this relationship as the union of two orphans, but it was most probably a lesbian relationship. Elflein, of course, never discusses her own sexuality, but she emboldens women to travel alone, "brave, enthusiastic, and happy!" (April 28). Elflein herself will always travel with her partner and lead women-only rock climbing and sailing excursions.[17]

Reading Elflein's travel texts, it is difficult to associate her with men of her generation such as Gálvez, Rojas, and Lugones, although she shares their preoccupation with nationality. In her textbooks and children's stories, Elflein strives to contribute to an educational project that would assimilate immigrant children into Argentinity. When one reads Elflein's nationalist texts, on the other hand, it is difficult to associate her with the first generation feminists such as Cecilia Grierson and Julieta Lanteri. It is only in the intersections of Elflein's textbooks and her travel books that we can account for her combined concerns with the homeland and the role of women in its history. Elflein contributes to the nationalist discourse with innumerable legends, traditions, and children's stories. She does, however, distance herself from the nationalists of the time vis-à-vis women's roles. In that area, Elflein's commitment to the normal school movement is unfaltering. What she presents in her texts, therefore, is a way to bare nationalist discourse of the reactionary and sexist elements that limit women's participation in public life.

Reading/Writing Margins

Elflein's descriptions, like Grierson's, echo those of Sarmiento, sometimes to the point of using the same words to describe the same regions. The whole collection of articles which make up her *Por campos serranos* is organized around the contrast between civilization and barbarism, city and country. Even the title of one of her books—*De tierra adentro*—exemplifies the economic organization of the pieces: Buenos Aires as the center, the provinces as "tierra adentro," the regions to which access from Buenos Aires required (still in 1918) a difficult and troublesome trip. The longer the trip from Buenos Aires and from the cities, the more the regions are described as enclosed areas, closed flowers which would bloom once the civilizing forces from Buenos Aires (especially normal schools and railways) opened them up. Elflein's trip is always narrated as a movement into the "interior" from the cities, the few cities as the point from which the less civilized interior—"adentro"—can be visited. And the city has "una atracción atávica" [an atavistic attraction], reversing the use that Sarmiento makes of the adjective: what is "atávico/a" in *Facundo* is the impulse toward barbarism, while in Elflein's writing, civilization has already triumphed and has become naturalized. Alerting her readers to the possibility of a relapse into barbarism, she includes a reference to the desert as exercising its primeval influences on her. This only stresses the power Sarmiento had bestowed on the desert: it could even corrupt an educated woman of European origin:

> Pronto dejamos atrás los pésimos caminos del ejido y nos hallamos en la campaña, donde según histórica frase política, todo suele ser camino. Atravesábamos la región mediterránea argentina típica: esa zona arenosa, espinosa, seca, en cuyo suelo podría caer el diluvio sin dejar huellas, donde el viento se calienta y el sol arde furioso, zona que en mí ha ejercido siempre una fascinación quizá atávica. (April 21)

> [Soon we leave behind us the terrible roads of the communal land and we find ourselves in the country where according to a historical political slogan everything is a road. We crossed the typical Argentinean Mediterranean region: that sandy, thorny, dry area on whose ground it could rain in torrents without leaving a trace; where the wind warms up and the sun blazes furiously, an area that has always exercised a perhaps atavistic fascination in me.]

In *Literatura autobiográfica argentina,* Adolfo Prieto argues that the interest in describing the Argentine scenery appeared in Argentina only after massive immigration. Unlike some of her contemporaries, Elflein's interest in the scenery and its inhabitants is undermined by her urge to see that scenery dramatically changed by the forces of civilization. Even if she agrees with criollista writers on the importance of the scenery in the definition of the national, she captures it in the process of being modified, of being interfered with. Unlike other writers whose contribution is depicting an unobliterated preindustrial landscape, she shows the landscape begging to be obliterated and included in capitalist exploitation. Elflein's travel writing interrupts the discourse of the vanishing country life since it actually shows it as still existent but quickly disappearing. This conflation of the extant and the disappearing is articulated by her through the use of conventions from older forms of travel writing and of Sarmiento's appropriations of this form. The very nature of the trip, from the cities into the landscape, from civilization into barbarism, is paradigmatic. Some parts of her narrative echo that of previous travelers:

> Por siglos ha caminado a través de nuestros campos la tropa de carretas y por siglos más caminará lenta, serena y pintoresca hasta que la vía férrea triunfe sobre ella. (April 17)

> [For centuries the troop of wagons have crossed our lands and for many more centuries they will cross, slowly, serenely and picturesquely until the railroad triumphs over them.]

Elflein also situates the "criollos" in an anachronistic situation vis-à-vis the rest of the country:

> La franqueza y generosidad con que los criollos de hace cien años recibían al forastero desconocido, allí subsisten, allí florecen hoy como hace un siglo. (April 21)

> [The frankness and generosity with which the creoles of a hundred years ago received unknown foreigners, there they subsist, there they flourish today like a century ago.]

If we remember the debate after the Campaign to the Desert to decide the nationality of the Indian populations, in which some congressmen had suggested considering them foreigners (see chapter 3), this definition of the criollos reiterates the elements of the debate. The criollos are Argentine-born but they are foreign inasmuch as they represent an older order. Travelers (Elflein, the British travelers to whom her "forastero desconocido" is a veiled allusion) have discursive authority over the criollos since they represent modernity and progress. As representatives of the metropolis (Europe, Buenos Aires), these travelers have the descriptive authority to represent these anachronistic beings. This authority is exemplified by Elflein's use of the naming trope, another convention of travel writing which allows the traveler to use his/her authority to confer names, to codify the world. Elflein does this by first showing how uninterested criollos were in codifying their own world:

> —¿Cómo se llama esta planta?

> —No sé io.

> —¿Y aquél árbol?

> —Arbol no más es el nombre. (May 13)

> [What's the name of this plant?

> I don't know.

> And that tree?

> It's just called tree.]

By another related strategy, Elflein appropriates phrases and expressions from the countryside and incorporates them into her text:

> El clima (según la expresión de una criollita que nos informó al respecto, en la región "llueve más mucho que poco") es sano y agradable sin extremos de calor ni de frío. (May 19)

[The climate (according to the expression of the creole girl who told us about it: in the area "it rains much more than little") is healthy and pleasant without extremes of heat or cold.]

The language from the interior becomes then a tokenistic expression of nationality in much the same way as the landscapes are incorporated into the national consciousness as marks of Argentinity.

Gender roles further illustrate the temporal distance between the time of the narrative and the perceived anachronism of the order which is narrated: "Parecíamos a veces," Elflein writes, "estar en un hogar colonial como lo describen los viajeros de otras épocas" (April 21) [Sometimes we seemed to be in colonial homes like the ones the travelers of other times describe]. Elflein then describes in detail being pampered and attended to, and she finishes the piece with a description of the siesta, the house closed, everyone inside in indolent abandon. The nostalgia that permeates the description, however, alerts the reader to the anomalous characteristic of this situation. The following piece on the same city—San Francisco del Monte—describes the counterpart of the placid situation described before: the normal school "en la que tantas esperanzas cifran los habitantes de San Francisco y de toda la campaña . . ." (April 28) [in which the residents of San Francisco and of all of the countryside place so much hope]. The anomalous nature of the placid siesta described is also stressed when, in one of the few asides specifically aimed at informing the reader of tourist options, the region is described as a nice place to spend "una temporada agradable" (April 28) [a pleasant time]. The departure from the tone is narrated in "modernista" prose which further distances San Francisco:

No se la tragó [the Fenris wolf] aquella noche, pues el disco luminoso [the moon] brillaba plácidamente sobre San Francisco, cuando nuestros caballos cruzaron al galope sus calles olfateando la querencia. (April 28)

[The Fenris wolf didn't swallow the moon that night, for the luminous disc shone placidly over San Francisco, while our horses galloped through its streets scenting out their home.]

The conflation of a German classic legend with the creole "querencia" serves to distance San Francisco more from the present time where Elflein situates herself. The horses, which replace the car Elflein and her friend use for most of the trip, are used metonymically to refer to Elflein and her friend, who use the energy and virility of the horses to distance themselves from the town where they were included in a colonial family organization, which was of course very limiting compared to the active space they inhabit as modern single women. The use of the noun "querencia" situates the narrative in an authentically criollo environment but also distances the time spaces further. "Querencia," a criollo version of melancholy, becomes something which is sensorially apprehended by the horses. It is a new expression of the melancholic state in which the undeveloped areas submerge Elflein. "Querencia" is therefore an Argentinean version of melancholy as well as an idiosyncratic symbol of belonging in the nation.

To escape melancholy, the cities from the interior have to follow the example of Buenos Aires. The interior is repeatedly referred to as melancholic, lacking the energy and life of Buenos Aires. The descriptions of these cities stress the lack of modernity:

> Pasada la primera impresión de interés que despierta todo lo nuevo, nos sentimos en la ciudad capital de la provincia, *invadidos por la melancolía* [emphasis added]. La edificación chata, las calles flanqueadas de tapias de adobe y sin aceras a dos pasos del centro, escasos y pobres los sitios de recreo, la catedral en el mismo estado semi-concluido en que dicen se hallaba hace veinte años, las calles vacías de gente, sin tranvías, y el conjunto dormido silencioso ... tal es San Luis.—¿No tiene vida esta ciudad?—preguntamos a amables vecinos y todos nos responden con la cohibición del enfermo que confiesa su mal:—No tiene ... (April 8)

> [After the initial interest that all new things awaken, we felt *invaded by melancholy* (emphasis added) in the capital city of the province. The flat construction, streets flanked with adobe walls and without sidewalks just a few steps from the center, scarce and poor recreation areas, the cathedral in the same half-finished state in which they say it was found twenty years ago, streets without people, without trams, and altogether asleep in silence ... so is San Luis. "Doesn't this city have any life?" we ask friendly neighbors and everyone answers with the restraint of the sick naming their ailment: "No it doesn't ...."]

I have already discussed how melancholy has been considered one of the ailments of the contact zone. In the nonmetropolitan areas, the metropolitan traveler is enslaved by the indolence and lack of activity prevalent in the region. Melancholy and indolence are always presented as gripping phenomena from which the metropolitan writer has to flee or run the risk of remaining forever trapped. This connotation of the word "melancholy" merges in the quotation above with another definition of the state coinciding also with colonialism: the "mal du siècle." In my section on Lina Beck-Bernard, I have discussed how she implicates the indigenous populations in this illness, how they become multivalent metaphors for colonialism, expansion, and disappearance. Elflein's description is at the intersection of the two definitions of melancholy: the city of San Luis is therefore described as producing melancholy in its visitors but also as melancholically waiting the demise of this melancholic state. Rather than explicitly prescribing the solution, Elflein voices it through the inhabitants (who are always referred to as "criollos"):

Pero otros decían:

...Por eso el puntano, en general,—aparte de ser, como todos los criollos, muy sobrio y de pocas necesidades—no siente estímulo ni acicate. Que vengan obras de irrigación, que vengan ferrocarriles....—Y que vengan muchos extranjeros—agregó otro caballero que se hallaba en la rueda.Y todos, al unísono repitieron:—¡Ah, sí! Que vengan muchos extranjeros sobre todo, con capital que es la fuente de las iniciativas. (April 8)

[But others say:

...That is the reason why the inhabitant of San Luis, in general—aside from being, like all creoles, very sober and with few needs—does not feel any stimulus or incentive. Let them bring irrigation works, let them bring railroads. . . . "And let them bring many foreigners" added another gentleman who found himself in the circle.And everyone repeated in unison:"Oh yes! Let them especially bring many foreigners, with their capital that is the source of initiative."]

This last sentence summarizes what Elflein puts forth as a model for Argentinity: the mythification of the hilly and desertic landscape of the interior that Sarmiento had blamed for being a source of barbarism, coupled with the modification of this landscape through the modernizing forces from the littoral. Elflein unequivocally suggests that the railways, the normal school system, and industrialization will put an end to the malaise-producing elements of the landscape.Yet she recovers them in writing; she codifies them and reserves them a place in the imaginary construction of the nation in which she so actively participated.

Elflein's travelogue, like the entire corpus of her writing, is didactically aimed at educating Argentineans in the glories of their history and the beauties of their country. It is therefore not surprising that a large part of her work is specifically produced to provide young readers with a code of landscapes and historical figures against which to trace their own national identity. Her project is different in tone and content but very similar in intent to that of the travel writer I treat in the next chapter: Delfina Bunge de Gálvez. Bunge was also a textbook writer and a writer of children's stories (as well as a poet, essayist, and autobiographer). Bunge's work, like Elflein's, is militantly didactic. The cause she champions is, however, quite different from Elflein's. Bunge attacks lay education and modernization, and her work expresses the need to reintegrate Catholicism into the nation as a defining element. It is not surprising, therefore, that although she traveled to Europe several times, she writes a travelogue on an experience in the Middle East. Set against Jews and Arabs as "others," Bunge celebrates the glories of Catholicism and calls the Catholic Church her "patria," the space where Bunge's definitions of her own identity did not have to include non-Catholics and even non-Christians. Written in the second half of the 1920s, Bunge's travelogue anticipates a reactionary and racist discourse which was at the heart of the insurrectionary military movement which in 1930 overthrew President Hipólito Irigoyen and initiated a cycle of military régimes that would mark the civil life of Argentina for the next fifty years.

8

The Spiritual Trip: Delfina Bunge de Gálvez's *Tierras del Mar Azul*

In *Viaje alrededor de mi infancia,* perhaps Delfina Bunge's most widely read book, there is an episode that is illuminating in the context of the present volume. Young Delfina is required by her teacher to write a travel account. Perplexed, the child decides to plagiarize from one of the travel books her father has written and published. The ploy is discovered and Delfina is punished. The episode is interesting because it points to several elements which are suggestive in an analysis of her work and of her time. The assignment in itself shows that the teacher was used to instructing students who were indeed exposed to traveling *en touriste.*[1] Delfina's response to the assignment—"¿Cómo de escribir sobre viajes yo que nunca he viajado?" [How can I write about travel if I've never traveled?]—is paradigmatic of the meaning of travel and traveling at the time. Bunge has indeed traveled before she is assigned this task: she spends her life between Buenos Aires and the family estancia, but she does not interpret this as traveling. Traveling is what she reads in the books her father and uncle wrote on going to Europe; for Bunge, the trips from the family *casona* in Buenos Aires to the family estancia in Córdoba are just another form of imma-nence, of immobility, an immobility which she will greatly praise in her *Viaje alrededor de mi infancia* and to which I will return later in the chapter. I will claim that by the end of her literary career, Bunge had not only written against the autobiographical tradition to which her *Viaje alrededor de mi infancia* belonged but had also subverted the forms of travel writing in Argentina with her *Tierras del mar azul.*

Tierras del mar azul is a travel book in which Bunge challenges modes of self-representation for women of the upper class in Argentina. With this text she also adds a site to the European trip: the Mediterranean and the Holy Land. By this very conscious gesture, Bunge includes religion in travel literature (she is the first woman to do so) and coins a landscape where anxieties about immigration appear in the form of an ethnographic study on Arab and Jewish customs. The travel book Delfina Bunge published during the 1920s about a trip taken in 1926 with her husband and her three children—*Tierras del mar azul*—is a description of a pilgrimage to Jerusalem through Brazil, African and Arab countries, and culminating in Rome. In *Memorias de la vida literaria,* Manuel Gálvez describes how he and his wife sold their house to take this trip because they needed a respite from life in Buenos Aires. Both Bunge and Gálvez were commissioned to write about the trip; Gálvez produced travel accounts for *Caras y Caretas,* Bunge for *La Prensa.* While both of them planned to have their accounts published in book form, only Bunge achieved this purpose. We can only speculate on the reasons, but I believe that the involvement both writers show with spiritual issues was more welcome in women than in men. In *Visto, oído y recordado,* Daniel García Mansilla (Eduarda Mansilla's son) claimed that he would never become an important figure in Argentina because he was related to Rosas and he was a Catholic. García Mansilla argued that the discourse of spirituality was not welcome in men, although by the 1920s it was becoming a privileged discourse for women. Most of Bunge's other prose works also advocate religiosity and spiritual growth and condemn social movements such as socialism and feminism for subverting the order of family life and leading to the spiritual depravation of women and young people.

Manuel Gálvez published a travel book called *El solar de la raza* (1913) early in his career. Like Bunge's *Tierras del mar azul, El solar* was an unconventional travel book because it was devoted to his trip to Spain and to glorifying Hispanism as well as Castilian culture, its spirituality, and its religious faith. One of the most outstanding characteristics of this travelogue is that it sets up Spain as the center of what should be the trip to Europe of the Argentinean elites. Together with Ricardo Rojas's *El alma española, El solar* reevaluates the role of Spain in the definition of Argentina.

Delfina Bunge's work goes one step further in reevaluating the role of Europe and the Middle East as others against whom to construct Argentina as an imagined community. The corpus of her work is very diverse and includes poetry written in French, textbooks, spiritual essays, her autobiographical *Viaje alrededor de mi infancia,* and her travel book *Tierras del mar azul.* The last two texts, *Viaje alrededor de mi infancia* and *Tierras del mar azul,* are autobiographical in different ways, and a comparison of them can serve to theorize the kind of subjectivity Bunge is putting forth in her later text. *Viaje alrededor de mi infancia* can be read together with other works by upper-class women written at approximately the same time. These texts idealize childhood and narrate the life of women of the upper class as an uninterrupted continuum of parties, social visits, and cultural diversions. In these texts, the personal is something to dwell on, to narrate in detail. These writings always include a thorough journey through the intricacies of family and blood relations. In *Tierras del mar azul,* in contrast, Bunge moves away from the conventions of the autobiographical into a text where ideas and ideology are explicitly privileged and the personal is erased in the process. Delfina Bunge, therefore, shares with the other travel writers in this chapter the type of impersonal discourse where the personal and the interior, characteristics par excellence of female travel writing, are completely absent. In Bunge's case, this anomaly not only marks a departure from the conventions of the genre but also a distancing from her own class status and from the kind of writing women in her social class produced at the time. Her writing on this trip is far less personal than that of her husband's, and she is the one who gets her travel accounts published as a book. Her work not only erases the personal in terms of family relationships and of accommodations but also in terms of her husband's literary successes. Whereas Gálvez dwells on the meetings with famous literary figures of the stature of Marinetti, Bunge presents herself as the anonymous traveler, deeply involved in the religious experience that traveling in non-Christian but biblical lands can afford her.

Bunge's travel book also challenges the premise that the traditional European trip of the Argentine elites is flawed because it appeals to the aesthetic and not the spiritual needs of the travelers:

> ¡Cuántos hay que van a Europa, cinco, seis veces, y no piensan jamás en ir a Jerusalem! Cristianos que no sueñan sino con Londres y con París. Son, sin duda, intensas las impresiones de arte que París o Londres pueden darnos. Pero, ¿es esto comparable con lo que en Palestina nos espera? (195)

> [How many go to Europe, five, six times, and never think of going to Jerusalem! Christians who dream but of London and Paris. Powerful indeed are the impressions of art that London and Paris can offer us. But, is this comparable with what awaits us in Palestine?]

Structured as the narration of a pilgrimage, the trip Bunge narrates starts in Brazil, takes her through the Mediterranean and the Middle East, and ends in Rome with the conflation of the two elements that Bunge sees as antithetic in the quotation above: the artistic and the spiritual. It is not surprising that what Bunge says about Rome is that

Yo sólo quise dar esta impresión de Patria que en Roma nos aguarda. Esta alegría de ser recibido como un hijo en el abrazo de las columnatas de San Pedro. (214)

[I only wanted to give this impression of fatherland that awaits us in Rome. This happiness of being welcomed like a son in the arms of Saint Peter's colonnades.]

This embrace is particularly suggestive if we read it in the context of another embrace Bunge had referred to before. In her description of "the old Cairo" as she calls it, she mentions a mosque with special characteristics:

Esto pasa cerca de la entrada, en una especie de patio que precede a la mezquita o forma parte de ella, y no lejos de dos columnas cercadas por alambres. Entre estas columnas, dice la leyenda, sólo puede pasar un hombre honrado, y han tenido que cercarlas por los muchos que, queriendo hacer alarde de honradez, han muerto apresados por ellas. (106)

[This takes place near the entrance, in a kind of courtyard that precedes the mosque or forms part of it, and not far from two wire fenced columns. Between these columns, goes the legend, only an honest man can pass; but they have had to close them off due to the many who, wanting to make a show of their honesty, have died in their grasp.]

It is interesting to note the contrast between the loving, embracing columns of Catholicism and the dangerous, murderous columns of Islam. In her trip, Bunge sets herself and what she considers Argentinean against two foreign peoples: Muslims and Jews. Her portrayal of both groups responds to very different prejudices. In her portrayal of Muslims, she echoes prevalent European views of Islam and Argentinean rewritings of these views which always associated Muslims with barbarism. In her portrayal of Jews, her discourse is imbued with the anti-Semitism of the contemporary nationalistic discourse in the country. Muslims are presented as metaphors for the barbaric elements within Argentina, Jews as an imminent danger to Argentinity as spirit.

Bunge's writing is defined by a hierarchy in which being Argentinean is associated with the past, with ancestry, and with a connection to the land, but, above all, with Catholicism. Bunge repeatedly uses the word "patria" to refer specifically to the motherland of the Catholic Church. Immigration is presented as a dissipating element which has brought on the current spiritual crisis of the country. It is therefore important to recover the spiritual elements, which is exactly what Bunge is doing in her trip to Jerusalem. Europe and the Middle East do not represent aesthetic pleasure for her but rather spiritual growth. The contrast between wealth and poverty, the economic and the spiritual, is at the forefront of her writings. Let us examine her judgment on possible immigrants:

Pienso que quizá alguno de estos pequeñuelos que ahora chapotean en el barro, con los pies descalzos se irá a probar fortuna a aquella ciudad que bien conozco.... ¿Qué le ofrecemos allí? El conventillo horrendo y la fábrica, con el solo respiradero del cinematógrafo norteamericano de deshecho (ladrones y "vampiresas"). Y cuando se haya civilizado tanto que sepa ya leer, se le venderán, por pocos centavos, revistas de un lodo más pernicioso, por cierto, que él de estas callejuelas. Y me entra una gran pena y el deseo de gritarle: "Quédate, pequeñuelo, aunque sea en las cercanías del Templo de Serapis; si en estas ruinas se oculta algún demonio adverso, mil otros te esperan en la gran ciudad.... No dejes que por un poquito menos de miseria material—¡y aún quién sabe!—tanta riqueza como estas tierras ofrecen a tu espíritu." (78–79)

[I think that perhaps one of these little ones, now splashing in the mud, with bare feet, will go and try his fortune in that city I know so well.... What do we offer him there? The horrible tenements and factory with the only respite of North American cinema in disarray (thieves and "vamps"). And when he has been civilized to the extent that he knows how to read, he will be sold, for a few cents, magazines of mud certainly more pernicious than that of the narrow streets. And I feel a great sorrow and the desire to yell to him: "Stay here, little one, even if near to the Temple of Serapis; if some adverse demon is hiding in these ruins, a thousand others await you in the big city.... Don't leave for a little less material misery—and who knows!— so much richness as this land offers your spirit."]

This portrayal of the life of the recent immigrants to Buenos Aires is populated by the stock images used by the incipient nationalistic movement: the "conventillo," lay culture, public education. The ironic reference to the forces of civilization envisioned by the generation of 1880, especially public education and its massive literary campaigns, is compared to the mud of the streets of Naples. The spirituality Bunge finds in her trip to Europe is contrasted with the worldliness and poverty of spirit she finds in Buenos Aires. Poverty is presented as dignified in Italy, where it is close to the origins of Western civilization, but as the source of evil and corruption of spirit in a lay (and heretic) society such as urban Argentina.

Muslims had been used by writers such as Sarmiento in comparisons with the gauchos. The gauchos and their culture were likened to nomadic Islamic groups in Palestine in a portrayal undoubtedly borrowed from French Romanticism. In Bunge's portrayal, however, Muslims represent barbarism because they are not Christian, and the gaucho is therefore absent from the comparison since by the time Bunge is writing, gauchos had already become canonized figures representing what was Argentinean in opposition to the foreignness of immigrants.

In Bunge's text, the narrative of self takes second place to the narrative of nationality, which is reinterpreted as a spiritual narrative. Bunge uses Orientalism, in Lisa Lowe's terms, "as a matter of cultural quotation, or of the repetition of cultural signs" (2). Her cultural reservoir includes French Romantic novels and Argentinean quotations of French Romantic Orientalisms. She concentrates, however, very specifically on what Arabs do in open spaces, neglecting completely the discourse of the interiors which seemed particularly attractive for other women travelers. There are no references to family relations and domestic arrangements in either her own world or in the places she visited.

Tierras del mar azul undermines the relevance of her own public life in an attempt to highlight her mission as a Catholic propagandist. Her book, however, could not be read as a compendium of gossip and travel suggestions like many travel books published at the time but rather as an invitation to join in the spiritual search of its writer.

As we have seen, the three travel writers I treat in this part of the book—Cecilia Grierson, Ada María Elflein, Delfina Bunge—do not fit into the characteristic delimitations of female travel writers: they do not write about the private or the "feminine," and their self-configuration is not carried out in terms of a "personal" self but rather in terms of a professional or a collective self. The mere existence of these texts bears testimony to changing attitudes in Argentina toward the professionalization of women and toward the strict division of public and private as the spaces of men and women. Cecilia Grierson fought for the opening up of public spaces for women. Ada Elflein gave these new female spaces a national content. Delfina Bunge added a religious element to the definition of nation and created a racist and reactionary discourse to resist the laity and the cosmopolitanism of the new nation. Even if in the 1930s her ideology gained momentum, it was ultimately doomed to failure, although some of its contents live uncomfortably on in the present.

Notes

Introduction

1. There are conflicting views regarding the veracity of the official version of Argentinean history that places the first singing of the national anthem in Mariquita Sánchez's soirée. Chilean painter Pedro Subercasseaux painted *El himno nacional en la sala de María Sánchez* for the hundredth anniversary of the May Revolution in 1910 basing his portrayal in the narration of the event that appeared in Pastor Obligado's *Tradiciones*. See Sáenz Quesada 64, 327.

2. For an analysis of the connections between different forms of subalternity, see Rodríguez (1996).

3. See Salessi.

4. See Clifford (1997), Pratt (1987), and Taussig.

5. Grewal ties the two terms to show how they functioned together within European colonialism: "Both 'home' and 'harem' are, I argue, relational nationalist constructs that require the deployment of women and female bodies within the antagonistic and comparative framework of colonial epistemology" (*Home and Harem* 5). Feminist scholars have been examining the complex relationship between women travelers as witnesses and participants in colonialism. See, for example, Chaudhuri and Strobel; Grewal and Kaplan; Lowe; and Mills.

6. See Prieto (1996) and Viñas (1971, 1998). Recent works on travel writing published in Argentina include Kupchik, Monteleone, and Szurmuk.

7. See Franco (1979).

8. Feminist scholars have been working on the role of gender in the construction of national identities in Latin America for more than a decade. See, for example, Fletcher (1994), Garrels (1987), Masiello (1992), Rodríguez (1994), and Sommer.

1. A House, a Home, a Nation: Mariquita Sánchez's
Recuerdos del Buenos Ayres Virreynal

1. See Ribera 298–99.

2. This letter is published in Sáenz Quesada's biography of Mariquita Sánchez,

Mariquita Sánchez: Vida política y sentimental. Laiseca's *Cartas de Mariquita Sánchez* contains the most thorough collection of Sánchez's correspondence.

3. Mariquita Sánchez traveled to Montevideo in 1838 and lived there off and on until 1852.

4. In José Mármol's *Amalia,* one of Argentina's foundational novels, for example, the scene that depicts the party includes an example of "bad poetry" penned and read by Mercedes Rosas de Rivera. To be a Federal poet was synonymous with being a "bad poet" and with lacking sensibility and aesthetic appreciation. By class extraction, Mercedes Rosas could have been a good poet, but her relationship with Rosas and the Federals ruined that possibility. The scene in *Amalia* also points to something else: Mármol, a staunch Unitarian, shows Rosas unsuccessfully trying to imitate a Unitarian event, producing a poet (and a female one at that) and appreciating poetry, when poetry and poetic sensibility were associated with the Romantic Unitarians.

5. Sánchez's mother opposed the marriage on economic grounds. Marriages between cousins were common and were encouraged by colonial society. The wealthy groom who had been selected by Sánchez's parents to marry their only daughter was much older than she. Sánchez's second marriage was as scandalous as her first. She married her daughters' piano teacher, seven years her junior, nine months after her first husband's death, and she gave birth to their first child seven months after the wedding. For more on Sánchez's private life, see the biography by María Sáenz Quesada.

6. Susan M. Socolow has analyzed the institutionalized procedure by which children could challenge their parents' opposition to an undesirable marriage in the colonies. For more information on the mechanics of the ecclesiastical procedure, see Martín 104–40. Both Socolow and Martín stress the increased flexibility of patterns of marriage in the Spanish colonies in contrast to Spain.

7. The level of unrest brought on by Camila O'Gorman's elopement with a priest and the seriousness this elopement had in the context of Rosas's government is symptomatic of the way in which the level of control a government had over its middle- and upper-class women was an index of its legitimacy. Drawing from the same discourse, Unitarians and Federals used the metaphor of the abducted daughter (a victim, undesiring, passive) and the fallen woman ad nauseam to discuss the ills of the nation. An article published in *El Mercurio de Chile* expresses this problematic very clearly:

> Ha llegado a tal extremo la horrible corrupción de las costumbres bajo la tiranía espantosa del "Calígula del Plata," que los impíos y sacrílegos sacerdotes de Buenos Aires huyen con las niñas de la mejor sociedad, sin que el infame sátrapa adopte medida alguna contra esas monstruosas inmoralidades. (Quoted by Enrique Molina)

> [The horrible corruption of customs under the tyranny of "Caligula of the Plata" has reached such an extreme that the impious and sacrilegious priests

of Buenos Aires Xee with the little girls of the best society without the infamous tyrant adopting any means against these monstrous immoralities.]

8. Sáenz Quesada's biography of Sánchez and recent publications on her writing by María Gabriela Mizraje have fostered a new interest in Sánchez as a more complex and less stereotypical historical figure.

9. Martín Thompson's father was an English Protestant, but he had supposedly converted to Catholicism after a religious experience at sea. By converting to Catholicism, he opened up for himself a career in business in Buenos Aires and military careers for his sons. In their analysis of *Recuerdos de provincia,* Altamirano and Sarlo point out how "judío" and "hereje" function as insulting equivalents of "extranjero" (1983: 188). It is interesting to speculate on the equation of foreignness and Jewishness, which will become so clear during the first half of the twentieth century.

10. Other women writers use the trope of the dark stranger, a threatening figure that is confused with an animal. In Emma de la Barra's *Stella* (discussed in chapter 6), for example, the "mushinga," a black child, scares angelic Stella who thinks the black child is a strange animal.

2. Queen of the Interior: Lina Beck-Bernard's *Le Rio Parana*

1. *L'estancia de Santa Rosa* was first published in the *Revue de Deux Mondes* in 1864. It was recently reprinted in Argentina in a bilingual edition funded by the National University of the Littoral and the Alliance Française.

2. For an insightful discussion of women-authored texts that resist the discourse of rape as the only possible way in which to narrate relationships between white women and Indians, see Rotker (1997, 1999).

3. For a discussion of antifigures in nineteenth-century French literature, see Lowe 77.

4. Her great-grandfather Conrad Pfeffel seems to have been the one who even after his death opened the doors of the literary world for her. References to her in French journals such as the *Revue de Deux Mondes* always highlight the importance of this ancestor who was responsible for her intellectual upbringing after the murder of her father by one of his workers. The circumstances of her father's tragic death also appear explicitly.

5. Ezequiel Gallo explains:

Diversas leyes se dictaron durante el período tendientes a estimular la colonización agrícola. Se entregó tierra a precios bajos, alguna vez gratuitamente, obligándose a quienes la recibían a subdividirla y a radicar familias de inmigrantes extranjeros en ellas. (*Pampa,* 38–39)

[Several laws were passed during the period to stimulate agrarian colonization. Land was granted at very low prices, even for free sometimes. Those who bought or were given pieces of land were forced to subdivide them and populate them with foreign immigrants.]

3. Eduarda Mansilla de García's *Recuerdos de Viaje:* "Recordar es Vivir"

1. "Recordar es Vivir" [To remember is to live] is the epigraph of Mansilla's *Recuerdos de viaje.*

2. For the British and American travelers, there was a further step: the owners of the land also had to work it—to make it productive, to include this land and its inhabitants in the production and exchange of capital. This argument was used to justify appropriation and exploitation.

3. Sommer uses these categories to talk about literary works, and I am using them to refer to "real-life characters," but considering how the lives of these historical figures were interwoven with the literary and political life of the country, I see this analysis as a productive means for discussing social relations too.

4. For a detailed analysis of the travel book tradition in Argentina, see Viñas, *De Sarmiento* 141–211, and Noé Jitrik's introduction to *Los viajeros.*

5. As a matter of fact, María Rosa Oliver wrote a book on the United States, *América vista por una mujer argentina* (1945), which is similar in tone to Eduarda Mansilla's even though it addresses practical issues of being a female tourist more directly.

6. In *Stella,* a best-seller from the beginning of the twentieth century that I will refer to in further detail in chapter 6, Emma de la Barra makes extensive use of the space of the family "estancia" and contrasts life in the "estancia" to life in the city. The "estancia" is used as a setting by women writers of this social class such as Beatriz Guido and Silvina Bullrich well into the 1970s and 1980s. Arturo Jauretche's discussion of Beatriz Guido's *Fin de fiesta* and *El incendio y las vísperas* in *El medio pelo en la sociedad argentina* analyzes the trope of the "estancia" and of the upper class's literary perceptions of space from a nationalist perspective.

7. Eduarda Mansilla could exorcise the past in a way that her brother Lucio V. could not do. Both Prieto (1966) and Molloy (1980, 1991) have studied the ways in which the ghosts of General Lucio Norberto Mansilla and of Juan Manuel de Rosas hovered around Lucio V. Mansilla and interfered with his possibilities of political success.

8. Buenos Aires became the capital of the country in 1880, and since the yellow fever epidemic in 1871, the city had been going through a gradual transformation from "la gran aldea" to a Paris-inspired metropolis. For a detailed description of this process, see Francisco Bullrich.

9. In *Visto, oído y recordado,* Mansilla's son, Daniel García Mansilla, devotes a few lines to the impressions his family had on their return to Paris in 1873 after their second stay in the United States:

> La capital de Francia presentaba todavía cicatrices de la derrota del 70 y de los graves incendios de la Commune. Las ruinas del Palacio de las Tullerías, con todas sus ventanas negras y quemadas, nos impresionaron hondamente. (122)

[The French capital still showed scars from the defeat of 70 and of the serious fires of the Commune. The ruins of the Palace of the Tuileries with all of its black and burned windows, deeply impressed us.]

10. See for example *Un amor*.

11. Whenever Mansilla writes about North American women, she insists on their whiteness, natural or obtained through the use of cosmetics:

En ninguna parte existe mayor variedad de blanco de perla, blanco de lirio, blanco de cisne, blanco de Venus, y de cuantos blancos puedan ocurrir a la imaginación fertilísima de un químico poeta, que en el drug store de los Estados Unidos. (122)

[Nowhere is there a greater variety of pearl white, iris white, swan white, Venus white, and of all the many whites that can occur to the fertile imagination of a chemist-poet, than in the drug store of the United States.]

4. Interlude in the Frontier: Lady Florence Dixie's *Across Patagonia*

1. This is often referred to as the ethnographic gaze.

2. According to Mary Louise Pratt, the "arrival scene" is a stock scene in travel narrative and a trope in the "language of conquest" ("Scratches" 35–37). Late-nineteenth-century travel narratives dwell on the arrival scene in narrative but do not include this scene in their sketches and, in turn, include sketches from where the describing viewer is absent. The reason for this exclusion might be that the visual similarity between sketches of conquest scenes (for example, of Columbus's landing) and the observer/scientist arriving is too disturbingly overt for the scientific nineteenth-century chroniclers who see themselves as writing against the tradition of conquest glorification.

3. Other sketches characteristic of the genre depict different activities in different sketches. The European observer is always absent. See, for example, the illustrations of Guinnard's account in the *Le Tour du Monde*.

4. Gayatri Spivak asserts that "[a] basic technique of representing the subaltern as such (of either sex) is as the object of the gaze 'from above'" ("A Literary Representation" 264).

5. Maybe this kind of comparison can be looked at as a precursor of the work of "Second Wave" feminist anthropologists who have, for some time, been using fieldwork among tribal groups to make generalizations on gender roles. In Dixie's case, there is never any overt declaration of why she is describing women.

6. Even the use of terms such as "husband," "wife," and "matrimony" is unusual. Most travel writers refer to this type of relationship among Indians as "mates" or "savage companions."

7. See Newton, Ryan, and Walkowicz.

5. Traveling/Teaching/Writing: Jennie Howard's
In Distant Climes and Other Years

1. For an analysis of how these contradictions played themselves out in the context of Argentina's political arena, see Guy.

2. It can be argued that Sarmiento could have saved himself many problems if he had selected Catholic teachers instead of Protestant ones. There were very few Catholic teachers among the ones hired by Sarmiento, and several of them ended up working for the upper-class ladies Sarmiento antagonized so much.

3. Howard's narrative is self-effacing except in the very instance in which it becomes the most racist and prejudicial. In the only instance in which Howard uses the pronoun "I," she does so to express her prejudices, which, for some reason, she is able to call more her own than any of the experiences or feelings she had in Argentina:

> In general, the Argentine teachers are lacking in the matter of discipline and punctuality, and it is more difficult for the Latin race to speak the truth, *I* am inclined to think, than it is for others. They also put off 'til tomorrow all things that can, would, or should be done today, so there were deeply grounded faults to be eradicated in the young teacher's training which will still take some generations to eradicate. (82)

4. Work outside the home was still seen as dangerous for women as late as the early 1900s and beyond. Women who worked outside the home were perceived as always one step away from prostitution, which was also defined as sex outside marriage.

5. This we do not know for sure, since she never makes specific reference to her own situation but to that of the American teachers in general.

6. Traveler/Governess/Expatriate: Emma de la Barra's *Stella*

1. Alex is presented as a member of another race: her dispute with her cousins is described as "[c]onflicto sin salida, porque se establecía entre personas que siendo de la misma sangre, no eran de la misma raza . . ." (161) [an unresolvable conflict because it was established between people who shared the same blood but were not of the same race . . .]

2. It is not clear where these virtues and values are supposed to come from. They include Christian virtue, a belief in hard work, and a romanticization of the spaces of simple life in the land.

7. Globe-Trotting Single Women

1. An exception to the internationalist spirit of the celebrations was the Congreso Patriótico de Señoras [Patriotic Conference of Ladies] presided over by Alvina Van Praet de Sala. This conference, organized by members of the National Council of Women, brought together mainly upper-class women from the traditional fami-

lies who were active in charity organizations. The hegemonic discourse in this conference was nationalistic with profuse references to the Hispanic past, to the heroes of independence, and to the need to revitalize the spiritual values of the nation.

2. Between the mid-nineteenth century and the mid-twentieth century, Argentina was the country which received the largest impact of European immigration in the world. In 1910, half the population of Buenos Aires was foreign-born. See Indec, and Korn.

3. I am echoing Carlos Altamirano's use of the term "foundation." See his "La fundación de la literatura argentina."

4. The use of "castellano" instead of "español" was a political decision. For the definitions of the terms of the debate, see Alonso.

5. Rojas and Gálvez were from the provinces, as were most of the other intellectuals of the "generation of *Ideas*." For a discussion of how the families and provinces of origin affected the construction of Rojas's and Gálvez's ideology, see Cárdenas and Payá.

6. In the 1940s, Gálvez went further in this direction with his revindication of Rosas and the "caudillos."

7. I am following here Masiello's analysis of Rojas's *Eurindia*. According to Masiello, Rojas's representation of women "looks back to preindustrial values, to an age when women were looked upon as the timeless yet silent protectors of state virtue. Both an inspiration and a reward for man, this female body provides an escape from the threats of modernity" (*Between* 140–41).

8. I have briefly referred to the problematic of prostitution in the period in chapter 5.

9. Alfonsina Storni translated Delfina Bunge de Gálvez's poetry from French to Spanish and was a friend of both Bunge and her husband, Manuel Gálvez. Storni—who, like Gálvez's Raselda, became pregnant out of wedlock—showed in her life how an economically independent woman could overcome the problems of such a situation. Unlike Raselda, she did not have an abortion but kept her son, raised him, and supported him.

10. For the development of normal schools as a professional option, see Tedesco, chapter 8. For a review of feminist movements at the beginning of the century, see Carlson, chapters 4 through 7.

11. Victoria Ocampo is the Argentine writer who writes most about the practice. See parts 1, 2, and 3 of her autobiography. The lack of mobility for women in Buenos Aires that Ocampo describes at length seems to have been class-determined. Researchers of the period stress the freedom of movement working-class and lower-middle-class women had in the period. See Korn, chapters 3 and 5, the introduction to Beatriz Sarlo's *El imperio de los sentimientos,* and chapter 3 of Sarlo's *Una modernidad periférica: Buenos Aires 1920–1930.*

12. Juana Paula Manso had also taken professional trips to investigate educational issues. A contemporary of Grierson, Julieta Lanteri, researched women's health in Europe between the years 1907 and 1920.

13. This essay, which Grierson read in the Liceo de Señoritas N. 1, is reproduced in its entirety in Taboada 127–40.

14. The new spirit is expressed in a memo Minister of Education Eduardo Wilde sent the principals of national schools in 1884:

> One teaches in the Argentinean Republic and for the Argentinean Republic and everything that the Republic is concerned with physically and morally has to be paramount in education. (Memo of Eduardo Wilde, minister of education, presented to Congress in 1883)

> [Se enseña en la República Argentina y para la República Argentina y es ella y todo lo que a ella interesa fisicamente y moralmente, lo que debe predominar en la enseñanza.]

15. This category of the adventurer—a single woman who travels unaccompanied by men and has fun attempting challenging excursions—had a long tradition in British travel writing by women. Much of the scholarship on British travel writers stresses the exceptional quality of these women travelers and their accomplishments.

16. All the articles from which I quote appeared in *La Prensa* during 1918. I will therefore include only the specific dates. These articles have also been published in my *Mujeres en viaje* 221–75.

17. I have developed this aspect of Elflein's work in more detail in "Ada María Elflein: Viaje al interior de las identidades."

8. The Spiritual Trip: Delfina Bunge de Gálvez's *Tierras del Mar Azul*

1. The teacher is none other than the omnipresent governess of the children of the rich. This same governess is also mentioned in Delfina's sister Julia's *Vida* and in Victoria Ocampo's autobiography. Between Bunge's and Ocampo's text we can reconstruct a list of students taught by the governess, which included President Roca's daughter.

Bibliography

Aitken, M. *A Girdle Round the Earth*. London: Constable, 1987.

Alexander, Sally. "Women, Class and Sexual Difference." *History Workshop* 17 (1984): 125–49.

Alonso, Amado. *Castellano, español, idioma nacional*. Buenos Aires: Coni, 1938.

Altamirano, Carlos, and Beatriz Sarlo. "La Argentina del centenario: Campo intelectual, vida literaria y temas ideológicos." *Hispamérica* 9, no. 25–26 (1980): 35–39.

———. "La fundación de la literatura argentina." In *Ensayos argentinos de Sarmiento a la vanguardia*. Ed. Carlos Altamirano and Beatriz Sarlo. Buenos Aires: Centro Editor de América Latina, 1983.

———. *Literatura/sociedad*. Buenos Aires: Hachette, 1983.

———. "¿Somos nación?" In *Ensayos argentinos de Sarmiento a la vanguardia*. Ed. Carlos Altamirano and Beatriz Sarlo. Buenos Aires: Centro Editor de América Latina, 1983.

Althusser, Louis. "Ideology and Ideological State Apparatuses." In *Lenin and Philosophy and Other Essays*. New York: Monthly Review Press, 1971.

Anderson, Benedict. *Imagined Communities*. London: Verso, 1983.

Anzoátegui, Ignacio B. *Manuel Gálvez*. Buenos Aires: Ediciones Culturales Argentinas, 1961.

Areán, Carlos. *La pintura en Buenos Aires*. Buenos Aires: Abel Resnik, 1981.

Armstrong, Nancy. "Literature as Women's History." *Genre* 20 (1987): 101–10.

Auza, Néstor Tomás. "Eduarda Mansilla: Escritora y mujer de su tiempo." In *Mujeres y escritura*. Ed. Mempo Giardinelli. Buenos Aires: Puro Cuento, 1989.

———. *Periodismo y feminismo en la Argentina*. Buenos Aires: Emecé, 1988.

Balderston, Daniel. "Introduction." In *The Historical Novel in Latin America*. Ed. Daniel Balderston. Gaithersburg, Md.: Hispámerica, 1986.

Barba, Enrique, et al. "La Campaña del desierto y el problema de la tierra: La ley de premios militares de 1885." In *Actas del segundo congreso de historia argentina y regional celebrado en comodoro Rivadavia del 12 al 15 de enero de 1973*. Buenos Aires, 1974. Vol. 3.

Barthes, Roland. *Camera Lucida: Reflections on Photography*. New York: Hill and Wang, 1981.

Bayer Osvaldo. *La Patagonia trágica*. Mexico: Nueva Imagen, 1980.

Beck-Bernard, Lina. *La estancia de Santa Rosa*. Santa Fe: Alianza Francesa y Universidad Nacional del Litoral, 1990.

———. *Le rio parana: Cinq années de séjour dans la république argentine*. Paris: Gressart, 1864.

Beerbohm, Julius. *Wanderings in Patagonia*. London: Chatto and Windus, 1981.

Benstock, Shari. *The Private Self: Theory and Practice of Women's Autobiographical Writing*. Chapel Hill: University of North Carolina Press, 1988.

Birkett, D. *Spinsters Abroad: Victorian Lady Explorers*. Oxford: Oxford University Press, 1989.

Bosch, Beatriz. "Patagonia y la cuestión de las tierras públicas en la confederación argentina." In *Actas del segundo congreso de historia argentina y regional celebrado en comodoro Rivadavia del 12 al 15 de enero de 1973*. Buenos Aires, 1974. Vol. 1.

Brintrup, Lilianet. *Viaje y escritura: Viajeros románticos chilenos*. New York: Peter Lang, 1992.

Bullrich, Francisco. "La arquitectura de Buenos Aires." In *La Argentina del ochenta al centenario*. Ed. Gustavo Ferrari and Ezequiel Gallo. Buenos Aires: Sudamericana, 1980.

Bunge, Julia Valentina. *Vida: Época maravillosa 1903–1911*. Buenos Aires: Emecé, 1965.

Bunge de Gálvez, Delfina. *En torno a León Bloy*. Buenos Aires: Club de Lectores, 1944.

———. *Tierras del mar azul*. Buenos Aires: Editorial América Unida, n.d.

———. *Viaje alrededor de mi infancia*. Buenos Aires: López, 1938.

Busaniche, José Luis. *Cinco años en la confederación argentina 1857–1862*. Buenos Aires: El Ateneo, 1935.

Butler, Judith. *Bodies That Matter: On the Discursive Limits of "Sex."* New York: Routledge, 1993.

———. *Gender Trouble: Feminism and the Subversion of Identity*. New York: Routledge, 1990.

Cárdenas, Eduardo José, and Carlos Manuel Payá. *El primer nacionalismo argentino*. Buenos Aires: Pena Lillo, 1978.

Carlson, Marifran. *Feminismo! The Women's Movement in Argentina from Its Beginnings to Eva Perón*. Chicago: Academy Chicago, 1988.

Chaudhuri, Nupur, and Margaret Strobel. *Western Women and Imperialism: Complicity and Resistance*. Bloomington: Indiana University Press, 1992.

Cirigliano, Gustavo. *Las maestras norteamericanas*. San Juan: Universidad Nacional de San Juan, 1988.

Clementi, Hebe. "La maestra normal, Raselda." In *Mujeres y Escritura*. Ed. Mempo Giardinelli. Buenos Aires: Puro Cuento, 1989.

Clifford, James. *The Predicament of Culture*. Cambridge: Oxford University Press, 1988.

————. *Routes: Travel and Translation in the Late Twentieth Century*. Cambridge: Harvard University Press, 1997.

Clifford, James, and G. E. Marcus. *Writing Culture: The Poetics and Politics of Ethnography*. Berkeley: University of California Press, 1986.

Cott, Nancy. "Passionlessness: An Interpretation of Victorian Sexual Ideology." *Signs* 4 (1978): 219–33.

De la Barra, Emma. *Stella*. Madrid: Hyspamérica, 1985.

De Lauretis, Teresa. *Alice Doesn't*. Bloomington: Indiana University Press, 1984.

Dixie, Florence. *Across Patagonia*. New York: R. Worthington, 1881.

Du Bois, Page. *Sowing the Body*. Chicago: University of Chicago Press, 1988.

Durnford, W. "Exploration of Central Patagonia." *Proceedings of the Royal Geographical Society of London* (1883): 84–89.

Elflein, Ada María. *Historias de luz y sombra*. Buenos Aires: Plus Ultra, 1984.

————. *Leyendas argentinas*. Buenos Aires: Huemul, 1986.

————. *De tierra adentro*. Buenos Aires: Hachette, 1961.

Fabian, Johannes. *Time and the Other: How Anthropology Makes Its Object*. New York: Columbia University Press, 1983.

Feijóo, María del Carmen. *Las feministas*. Buenos Aires: Centro editor de América Latina, 1975.

————. "La mujer en la historia argentina." *Todo es Historia* 183 (August 1982): 8–16.

Ferrari, Gustavo, and Ezequiel Gallo, eds. *La Argentina del ochenta al centenario*. Buenos Aires: Sudamericana, 1980.

Fiol-Mata, Licia. "The 'School-Teacher of America': Gender, Sexuality, and Nation in Gabriela Mistral." In *Queer Readings, Hispanic Writings*. Ed. Emilie Bergmann and Paul Julian Smith. Durham: Duke University Press, 1995.

Fletcher, Lea. *Una mujer llamada Herminia*. Buenos Aires: Catálogos, 1987.

Fletcher, Lea, ed. *Mujeres y cultura en la Argentina del siglo XIX*. Buenos Aires: Feminaria, 1994.

Foucault, Michel. *The Archaeology of Knowledge*. New York: Pantheon, 1972.

Franco, Jean. "Beyond Ethnocentrism: Gender, Power and the Third World Intelligentsia." In *Marxism and the Interpretation of Culture*. Ed. Lawrence Grossberg and Cary Nelson. Champaign-Urbana: University of Illinois Press, 1988.

————. "Killing Nuns, Priests, Women and Children." In *On Signs*. Ed. Marshall Blonsky. Baltimore: Johns Hopkins University Press, 1985.

————. "Self-Destructing Heroines." *Minnesota Review* 22 (1984): 105–15.

————. Prologue to *La tierra púrpura y allá lejos y hace tiempo*. Caracas: Biblioteca Ayacucho, 1980.

————. "Trends and Priorities for Research on Latin American Literature." *Ideologies and Literature* 4, no. 16 (May–June 1983): 107–20.

———. "Un viaje poco romántico: Viajeros británicos hacia sudamérica: 1818–1828." *Escritura: Revista de Teoría y Crítica Literaria* 4, no. 7 (1979): 129–42.

Furlong, Guillermo. "La Patagonia en la cartografía antigua y moderna." In *Actas del segundo congreso de historia argentina y regional celebrado en comodoro Rivadavia del 12 al 15 de enero de 1973.* Buenos Aires, 1974. Vol. 2.

Gallo, Ezequiel. *La pampa gringa.* Buenos Aires: Sudamericana, 1983.

Gálvez, Lucía. *Mujeres de la conquista.* Buenos Aires: Planeta, 1990.

Gálvez, Manuel. *El diario de Gabriel Quiroga.* Buenos Aires: Moen, 1910.

———. *La maestra normal.* Buenos Aires: Tor, 1914.

———. *Nacha Regules.* 1918. Buenos Aires: Losada, 1950.

———. *El solar de la raza.* Madrid: Saturnino Calleja, 1913.

———. *La trata de blancas.* Diss. Universidad de Buenos Aires. Buenos Aires: Imprenta de José Tragant, 1905.

García Mansilla, Daniel. *Visto, oído y recordado.* Buenos Aires: Guillermo Kraft, 1950.

Garrels, Elizabeth. "El 'espíritu de la familia' en *La novia del hereje de Vicente Fidel López.*" *Hispamérica* 16, no. 46–47 (1987): 3–24.

———. "Sarmiento and the Question of Woman: From 1839 to *Facundo.*" In *Sarmiento: Author of a Nation.* Ed. Tulio Halperín Donghi, Gwen Kirkpatrick, and Francine Masiello. Berkeley: University of California Press, 1994.

Gates, Henry Louis, Jr. "Introduction: Writing 'Race' and the Difference It Makes." In *"Race," Writing, and Difference.* Ed. Henry Louis Gates, Jr. Chicago: University of Chicago Press, 1985.

Gorriti, Juana Manuela. "Un año en California." *La revista de Buenos Aires* 18 (1986): 106–16, 228–41, 356–98.

———. *La cocina eclética.* 1877. Buenos Aires: Librería Sarmiento, 1977.

———. *Oasis en la vida.* Buenos Aires: Félix Lajouane, 1888.

———. *Panorama de la vida.* Buenos Aires: Librería e Imprenta de Mayo, 1876.

———. *Sueños y realidades.* Buenos Aires: Imprenta de Mayo de C. Casavalle, 1865.

———. *La tierra natal.* Buenos Aires: Félix Lajouane, 1889.

———. *Las veladas literarias de Lima, 1876–1877.* Buenos Aires: Imprenta Europea, 1892.

Greenstein, Susan. "Sarah Lee: The Woman Traveller and the Literature of Empire." In *Design and Intent in African Literature.* Ed. Dorsey, Egeruju, and Arnold. Washington, D.C.: Three Continents Press, 1979.

Grewal, Inderpal. *Home and Harem: Nation, Gender, Empire, and the Cultures of Travel.* Durham: Duke University Press, 1996.

Grewal, Inderpal, and Caren Kaplan, eds. *Scattered Hegemonies: Postmodernism and Transnational Feminist Practices.* Minneapolis: University of Minnesota Press, 1994.

Grierson, Cecilia. *Educación técnica de la mujer.* Buenos Aires: Tipografía de la Peninteciaría, 1902.

Guerra, Rosa. *Lucía Miranda*. Buenos Aires: Universidad de Buenos Aires, 1956.

Guinnard, Auguste. "Trois années de captivité chez les patagons." *Le Tour du Monde* (1856): 241–68.

———. *Trois années d'éclavage chez les patagons: Récit de ma captivité*. Paris: E. Brunet, 1864.

Gunn, J. "Recent Explorations in Tierra del Fuego." *Scottish Geographical Magazine* 4 (1888): 310–26.

Guy, Donna. *Sex and Danger in Buenos Aires*. Lincoln: University of Nebraska Press, 1991.

Halperín Donghi, Tulio. *Una nación para el desierto argentino*. Buenos Aires: Capítulo, 1982.

Hamalian, Leo. *Ladies on the Loose: Women Travellers of the Eighteenth and Nineteenth Centuries*. New York: Dodd, Mead, 1981.

Hernando, Diana. "*Casa y Familia*: Spatial Biographies in Nineteenth-Century Buenos Aires." Ph.D. diss. University of California, Los Angeles, 1973.

Howard, Jennie. *In Distant Climes and Other Years*. Buenos Aires: American Press, 1931.

Hudson, William Henry. *Idle Days in Patagonia*. New York: Dutton, 1917.

———. *The Purple Land*. New York: Modern Library, 1884.

———. *La tierra púrpurea y allá lejos y hace tiempo*. Caracas: Biblioteca Ayacucho, 1980.

Iglesia, Cristina, and Julio Schvartzman. *Cautivas y misioneros: Mitos blancos de la conquista*. Buenos Aires: Catálogos, 1987.

Indec. *La población no nativa de la Argentina*. Buenos Aires: Serie Análisis Demográfico #6.

Jauretche, Arturo. *El medio pelo en la sociedad argentina: Apuntes para una sociología nacional*. Buenos Aires: Corregidor, 1991.

Jitrik, Noé. "De la historia a la escritura: Predominios, disimetrías, acuerdos en la novela histórica latinoamericana." In *The Historical Novel in Latin America*. Ed. Daniel Balderston. Gaithersburg, Md.: Hispámerica, 1986.

———. *El 80 y su mundo*. Buenos Aires: Jorge Alvarez, 1968.

———. *Los viajeros*. Buenos Aires: Jorge Alvarez, 1969.

Kaplan, Cora. *Sea Changes: Culture and Feminism*. London: Verso, 1986.

Katra, William H. "Re-reading *Viajes*: Race, Identity, and National Destiny." In *Sarmiento: Author of a Nation*. Ed. Halperín Donghi, Jaksic, Kirkpatrick, Masiello. Berkeley: University of California Press, 1994.

Kirkpatrick, Gwen. "The Journalism of Alfonsina Storni: A New Approach to Women's History in Argentina." In Seminar on Feminism in Latin America, *Women, Politics, and Culture in Latin America*. Berkeley: University of California Press, 1990.

Kirkpatrick, Susan. *Las Románticas: Women Writers and Subjectivity in Spain, 1835–1850*. Berkeley: University of California Press, 1989.

Korn, Francis. *Buenos Aires: Los huéspedes del 20*. Buenos Aires: Grupo Editor Latinoamericano, 1989.

Kristeva, Julia. *Strangers to Ourselves*. New York: Columbia University Press, 1991.

Kupchik, Christian. *La ruta argentina: El país contado por viajeros y escritores*. Buenos Aires: Planeta, 1999.

Ladaga, Liliana R. "Contribución al estudio de la actividad parlamentaria en torno a los ferrocarriles patagónicos." In *Actas del segundo congreso de historia argentina y regional celebrado en comodoro Rivadavia del 12 al 15 de enero de 1973*. Buenos Aires, 1974.

Lafleur, Héctor René, and Sergio Provenzano. *Las revistas literarias argentinas (1893–1960)*. Buenos Aires: Eds. Culturales Argentinas, 1962.

Laiseca, Clara V. *Cartas de Mariquita Sánchez*. Buenos Aires: Peuser, 1952.

Levy, Jim. *Juana Manso, Argentine Feminist*. La Trobe University Institute of Latin American Studies, Occasional Papers no. 1. Boondora: La Trobe University Press, 1977.

Little, Cynthia. "Education, Philanthropy, and Feminism: Components of Argentine Womanhood, 1860–1926." In *Latin American Women: Historical Perspectives*. Ed. Asunción Lavrín. Westport, Conn.: Greenwood Press, 1978: 235–53.

———. "The Society of Beneficence in Buenos Aires, 1823–1900." Ph.D. diss. Temple University, 1980.

Lombroso, Gina. *The Soul of Woman*. New York: Dutton, 1923.

Lowe, Lisa. *Critical Terrains: French and British Orientalisms*. Ithaca: Cornell University Press, 1991.

Ludmer, Josefina. *El género gauchesco: Un tratado sobre la patria*. Buenos Aires: Sudamericana, 1988.

———. "Tretas del Débil." In *La sarten por el mango: Encuentro de escritoras latinoamericanas*. Ed. Patricia Elena González and Eliana Ortega. Río Piedras, Puerto Rico: Ediciones Huracán, 1984.

Lugones, María. "Playfulness, 'World'-Traveling, and Loving Perception." In *Haciendo caras/Making Face, Making Soul*. Ed. Gloria Anzaldúa. San Francisco: Aunt Lute, 1990.

Luiggi, Alice Houston. *Sixty-Five Valiants*. Gainesville: University of Florida Press, 1965.

Manganiello, Ethel M. *Historia de la educación argentina*. Buenos Aires: Librería del Colegio, 1980.

Mansilla, Eduarda. *Un amor*. Buenos Aires: El diario, 1885.

———. *Cuentos*. Buenos Aires: Imprenta de la República, 1880.

———. *Lucía Miranda: Novela histórica*. Buenos Aires: Juan A. Alsina, 1882.

———. *El médico de San Luis*. Buenos Aires: Eudeba, 1962.

———. *Pablo ou la vie dans les pampas*. Paris: E. Lachaud, 1869.

———. *Recuerdos de viaje*. Buenos Aires: Juan A. Alsina, 1880.

Mármol, José. *Amalia*. Buenos Aires: Centro Editor de América Latina, 1967.

Martín, Luis. *Daughters of the Conquistadores*. Albuquerque: University of New Mexico Press, 1983.

Martínez Estrada, Ezequiel. *Los invariantes históricos en el Facundo.* Buenos Aires: Casa Pardo, 1974.

———. *El mundo maravilloso de Guillermo Enrique Hudson.* Mexico: Fondo de Cultura Económica, 1971.

Masiello, Francine. "Between Civilization and Barbarism: Women, Family and Literature in Mid-Nineteenth Century Argentina." In *Cultural and Historical Grounding for Hispanic and Luso-Brazilian Feminist Literary Criticism.* Ed. Hernán Vidal. Minneapolis: Institute for the Study of Ideologies and Literature, 1989.

———. *Between Civilization and Barbarism: Women, Nation, and Literary Culture in Modern Argentina.* Lincoln: University of Nebraska Press, 1992.

———. "Contemporary Argentine Fiction: Liberal (Pre)Texts in a Reign of Terror." *Latin American Research Review* 16, no. 1 (1981): 218–25.

———. "Women, State, and Family in Latin American Literature of the 1920s." In *Seminar on Feminism and Latin American Culture, Women, Politics, and Culture in Latin America.* Berkeley: University of California Press, 1990.

McGann, Thomas F. "La Argentina y los Estados Unidos: 1880–1914." In *La Argentina del ochenta al centenario.* Ed. Gustavo Ferrari and Ezequiel Gallo. Buenos Aires: Sudamericana, 1980.

McGee Deutsch, Sandra. *Counterrevolution in Argentina, 1900–1932: The Argentine Patriotic League.* Lincoln: University of Nebraska Press, 1986.

Mills, Sara. *Discourses of Difference: An Analysis of Women's Travel Writing and Colonialism.* London: Routledge, 1991.

Mizraje, María Gabriela. *Argentinas de Rosas a Perón.* Buenos Aires: Biblos, 2000.

Molina, Enrique. *Una sombra donde sueña Camila O'Gorman.* Buenos Aires: Losada, 1973.

Molloy, Sylvia. *At Face Value: Autobiographical Writing in Latin America.* Cambridge: Cambridge University Press, 1991.

———. "Imagen de Mansilla." In *La Argentina del ochenta al centenario.* Ed. Gustavo Ferrari and Ezequiel Gallo. Buenos Aires: Sudamericana, 1980.

Monteleone, Jorge. *El relato de viaje: De Sarmiento a Umberto Eco.* Buenos Aires: El Ateneo, 1998.

Moreira de Alba, Beatriz, and Ana Inés Ferreira. "La patagonia a través de los mensajes presidenciales 1810–1930." In *Actas del segundo congreso de historia argentina y regional celebrado en comodoro Rivadavia del 12 al 15 de enero de 1973.* Buenos Aires, 1974. Vol. 3.

Muschietti, Delfina. "Mujeres que escriben: Aquel reino anhelado, el reino del amor." *Nuevo Texto Crítico* 3, no. 4 (1989): 79–102.

Navarro, Marysa. *Los nacionalistas.* Buenos Aires: Jorge Alvarez, 1968.

Newton, Judith L., Mary P. Ryan, and Judith R. Walkowicz. *Sex and Class in Women's History.* London: Routledge and Kegan Paul, 1983.

Novoa, Adriana Inés. "Unclaimed Fright: Race, Masculinity, and National Identity in Argentina 1850–1910." Ph.D. diss. University of California, San Diego, 1998.

Ocampo, Victoria. *Autobiografía*. Madrid: Alianza, 1991.

Onega, Gladys. *La inmigración en la literatura argentina (1880–1910)*. Rosario: Facultad de Filosofía y Letras, Cuadernos de Letras, 1965.

Piglia, Ricardo. "Ficción y política en la literatura argentina." *Cuadernos Hispanoamericanos: Revista Mensual de Cultura Hispanica* 517–19 (July–September 1993): 514–16.

Potter, Anne Louise. "Political Institutions, Political Decay and the Argentine Crisis of 1930." Ph.D. diss. Stanford University, 1979.

Pratt, Mary Louise. "Conventions of Representation: Where Discourse and Ideology Meet." In *Contemporary Perceptions of Language: Interdisciplinary Dimensions*. Ed. Heidi Byrnes. Washington: Georgetown University Press, 1982.

———. "Fieldwork in Common Places." In *Writing Culture: The Poetics and Politics of Ethnography*. Ed. James Clifford and George Marcus. Berkeley: University of California Press, 1987.

———. *Imperial Eyes: Travel Writing and Transculturation*. London: Routledge, 1992.

———. "Mapping Ideology: Gide, Camus and Algeria." *College Literature* 8 (1981): 158–74.

———. "Scratches on the Face of the Country: What Mr. Barrow Saw in the Land of the Bushman." In *"Race," Writing, and Difference*. Ed. Henry Louis Gates, Jr. Chicago: University of Chicago Press, 1985.

Prieto, Adolfo. *El discurso criollista en la formación de la Argentina moderna*. Buenos Aires: Sudamericana, 1988.

———. *La literatura autobiográfica argentina*. 1966. Buenos Aires: Centro editor de América Latina, 1982.

———. *Los viajeros británicos y la formación de la literatura argentina*. Buenos Aires: Sudamericana, 1996.

Primer congreso femenino internacional de la república Argentina. Asociación Universitarias Argentinas. Buenos Aires: Ceppi, 1911.

Primer congreso patriótico de señoras en América del Sud. Buenos Aires: Imprenta Europea de M. A. Rosa, 1910.

Rama, Angel. *La ciudad letrada*. Hanover: Ediciones del Norte, 1984.

———. *Los gauchipolíticos rioplatenses*. Buenos Aires: Centro Editor de América Latina, 1982.

———. "La modernización literaria latinoamericana." *Hispamérica* 36 (December 1983): 1–19.

Ramos, Juan P. *Historia de la instrucción primaria en la república Argentina 1810–1910*. Buenos Aires, 1910.

Ribera, Adolfo Luis. *El retrato en Buenos Aires 1580–1870*. Buenos Aires: Universidad de Buenos Aires, 1982.

Rivière, Joan. "Womanliness as a Masquerade." In *Formations of Fantasy.* Ed. Victor Burgin, James Donald, and Cora Kaplan. London: Methuen, 1986.

Rodríguez, Ileana. *House, Garden, Nation: Space, Gender, and Ethnicity in Postcolonial Latin American Literatures by Women.* Durham: Duke University Press, 1994.

———. *Women, Guerrillas, and War: Understanding War in Central America.* Minneapolis: University of Minnesota Press, 1996.

Rodríguez Pérsico, Adriana. *Un huracán llamado progreso: Utopía y autobiografía en Sarmiento y Alberdi.* Washington: Organización de los Estados Americanos, 1996.

Rojas, Ricardo. *El alma española.* Valencia: Sempere y Compañía, 1908.

———. *La argentinidad.* Buenos Aires: La Facultad, 1916.

———. *Blasón de plata.* 1910. Madrid: Hyspamérica, 1986.

———. *La restauración nacionalista.* Buenos Aires: Ministerio de Justicia, 1909.

Romero, José Luis. *El desarrollo de las ideas en la Argentina del siglo XX.* Mexico: Fondo de Cultura Económica, 1965.

Rosman-Askot, Adriana. "Out of the Shadows: Two Centuries of Argentine Women's Voices." *Critical Matrix* 2 (Spring 1986): 70–100.

Rotker, Susana. *Cautivas: Olvidos y memoria en la Argentina.* Buenos Aires: Ariel, 1999.

———. "*Lucía Miranda* negación y violencia del origen." *Revista Iberoamericana* 178–79 (1997): 115–27.

Rubin, Gayle. "The Traffic of Women: Notes on the 'Political Economy' of Sex." In *Toward an Anthropology of Women.* Ed. Rayna Reiter. New York: Monthly Review Press, 1975.

Ruiz, Elida. "Una reflexión sobre Juana Manso." In *Mujeres y escritura.* Ed. Mempo Giardinelli. Buenos Aires: Puro Cuento, 1989.

Sáenz Quesada, María. *Mariquita Sánchez: Vida política y sentimental.* Buenos Aires: Sudamericana, 1995.

Said, Edward. *Orientalism.* New York: Vintage, 1979.

———. "Orientalism Reconsidered." *Cultural Critique* (Fall 1985): 89–107.

Salessi, Jorge. *Médicos, maleantes y maricas: Higiene, criminología y homosexualidad en la construcción de la nación Argentina (Buenos Aires: 1871–1914).* Rosario: Beatriz Viterbo Editora, 1995.

Sánchez, Mariquita. *Recuerdos del Buenos Aires virreynal.* Buenos Aires: Ene, 1953.

Santos Gómez, Susana. *Bibliografía de viajeros a la Argentina.* Buenos Aires: FECIC, 1983.

Sarlo, Beatriz. *El imperio de los sentimientos.* Buenos Aires: Catálogo, 1985.

———. *Una modernidad periférica: Buenos Aires 1920 y 1930.* Buenos Aires: Nueva Visión, 1988.

———. "Vanguardia y vida literaria." In *Ensayos argentinos de Sarmiento a la vanguardia*. Ed. Carlos Altamirano and Beatriz Sarlo. Buenos Aires: Centro Editor de América Latina, 1983.

Sarmiento, Domingo Faustino. *Educación popular*. Buenos Aires: Librería La Facultad, 1915.

————. *Facundo*. Buenos Aires: Huemul, 1978.

————. *Viajes*. Buenos Aires: Editorial de Belgrano, 1981.

Scobie, James R. *Argentina: A City and a Nation*. 2d ed. New York: Oxford University Press, 1971.

————. *Buenos Aires: Plaza to Suburb*. New York: Oxford University Press, 1974.

Seminar on Feminism and Culture in Latin America. *Women, Culture, and Politics in Latin America*. Berkeley: University of California Press, 1990.

Shattock, Joanne. "Travel Writing Victorian and Modern: A Review of Recent Research." *Prose Studies* 5, no. 1 (1982): 151–64.

Shumway, Nicolas. *The Invention of Argentina*. Berkeley: University of California Press, 1991.

Smith-Rosenberg, Carroll. "Writing History: Language, Class and Gender." In *Feminist Studies/Critical Studies*. Ed. Teresa de Lauretis. Bloomington: Indiana University Press, 1986.

Socolow, Susan M. "Cónyuges aceptables: La elección de consortes en la Argentina colonial, 1778–1810." In *Sexualidad y matrimonio en la América hispánica: Siglos XVI–XVIII*. Ed. Asunción Lavrín. Mexico: El Colegio de México, 1991.

Soler, Ricaurte. *El positivismo argentino*. Mexico: Unam, 1979.

Sommer, Doris. *Foundational Fictions: The National Romances of Latin America*. Berkeley: University of California Press, 1991.

Sosa de Newton, Lily. *Las argentinas de ayer a hoy*. Buenos Aires: Zanetti, 1967.

Spivak, Gayatri Chakravorty. "A Literary Representation of the Subaltern: A Woman's Text from the Third World." In *In Other Worlds*. London: Routledge, 1987.

————. "Three Women's Texts and a Critique of Imperialism." *Critical Inquiry* 12 (1985): 262–81.

Steele, Cynthia. "Toward a Socialist Feminist Criticism of Latin American Literature." *Ideologies and Literature* 4, no. 16 (May–June 1983): 323–29.

Stolen, Kristi Anne. *The Decency of Inequality: Gender, Power and Social Change on the Argentine Prairie*. Oslo, Norway; Cambridge, Mass.: Scandinavian University Press, 1996.

Szurmuk, Mónica. "Ada María Elflein: Viaje al interior de las identidades." *Monographic Review/Revista Monográfica* 12 (1996): 337–44.

————. *Mujeres en viaje: Escritos y testimonios*. Buenos Aires: Alfaguara, 2000.

Taboada, Asunción. *Vida y obra de Cecilia Grierson, la primera médica argentina*. Buenos Aires: Triada, 1983.

Taussig, Michael. *Shamanism, Colonialism, and the Wild Man: A Study in Terror and Healing*. Chicago: University of Chicago Press, 1987.

Tedesco, Juan Carlos. *Educación y sociedad en la Argentina 1880–1945*. Buenos Aires: Solar, 1986.

Tinling, Marion. *Women into the Unknown: A Sourcebook on Women Explorers and Travelers*. New York: Greenwood, 1989.

Traba, Marta. "Hipótesis sobre una escritura diferente." *Quimera* 13 (1981): 9–11.

Trifili, Samuel. *La Argentina vista por viajeros ingleses 1800–1860*. Buenos Aires: Guré, 1959.

Ulla, Noemí. *La revista "Nosotros."* Buenos Aires: Galerna, 1969.

Uriburu, José Evaristo. *La República Argentina a través de las obras de los escritores ingleses*. Buenos Aires: Claridad, 1948.

Vásquez Presedo, Vicente. In *Estadísticas históricas argentinas (comparadas)*. Buenos Aires: Macchi, 1971.

Veyne, Paul. *Comment on écrit l'histoire*. Paris: Seuil, 1978.

Viñas, David. *Indios, ejércitos y fronteras*. Mexico: Siglo Veintiuno, 1982.

———. *Literatura argentina y realidad política: De Sarmiento a Cortázar*. Buenos Aires: Siglo XX, 1971.

———. *De Sarmiento a Dios: Viajeros argentinos a USA*. Buenos Aires: Sudamericana, 1998.

Walker, John. "Home Thoughts from Abroad." *Canadian Review of Comparative Literature* (1983): 333–76.

Williams, Raymond. *The Country and the City*. New York: Oxford University Press, 1973.

Williams Alzaga, Enrique. *La pampa en la novela argentina*. Buenos Aires: Estrada, 1955.

Wilson, Jason. *W. H. Hudson: The Colonial's Revenge*. London: University of London Institute of Latin American Studies, Working Papers, 1981.

Zavalía Lagos, Jorge. *Mariquita Sánchez y su tiempo*. Buenos Aires: Plus Ultra, 1986.

Index

Mónica Szurmuk is assistant professor of Latin American literature at the University of Oregon. She is the author of *Mujeres en viaje: Escritos y testimonios* (Buenos Aires: Alfaguara, 2000).